COURAGEOUS
Woman

Casting Cares Upon Jesus

CARMEN K. MAENDEL

DEDICATION

I would like to first dedicate this book to God the Holy Spirit, inside me, as He guides and directs my path every day of my life. None of this would be possible without God.

Proverbs 3:5-6—

"Trust in the Lord with all your heart and lean not on your own understanding. Acknowledge Him in all ways, and He will direct your path."

I also would like to dedicate this book to my husband, Nate Maendel, son, Josh Maendel, my mother, Ann Ellsworth, my mother-in-law, Annie Maendel, and sister-in-law, Louisa Decent, who have been my biggest support system ever, and to all the women who so openly shared their personal stories with me to glorify Jesus Christ and make this book truly special to share with everyone.

Thank you, Hanna Olivas, for your amazing support and encouragement along the way!

Special thanks also to James Allen, Mercile Martinsen, Dean Graziosi, Tony Robbins, and Armin Shafee for your incredible coaching/mentorship and helping me break through fears and barriers that would have prevented me from ever writing this book.

FOREWORD

By Hanna Olivas

There are some books that speak to the mind.

Others that stir the heart.

And then there are those rare, sacred books that awaken the soul.

Courageous Woman: Casting Cares Upon Jesus is one of those books.

From the moment I met Carmen Maendel, I knew I was in the presence of someone truly set apart. Her faith isn't just something she talks about; it's something she lives, breathes, and pours into others with humility, conviction, and joy. This book is a direct reflection of that spirit.

What Carmen has done here is nothing short of extraordinary. She has taken her own journey, her deeply rooted relationship with Jesus Christ, and paired it with the authentic, raw, and powerful stories of other women who have faced hardship, heartache, and hard seasons—and come out on the other side with unshakable faith. This is not a book of polished perfection. It's a book of holy surrender. It's courageous. It's emotional. It's deeply honest. And it is exactly what the world needs right now.

In a world full of noise and surface-level inspiration, Courageous Woman invites us into the sacred space of testimony. It's a reminder that God is still in the business of healing, redeeming, and transforming lives. These stories will make you weep, rejoice, and most of all believe.

Carmen's heart is one of service, love, and boldness. Her willingness to lift other women up, to shine a light on their journeys, and to do so through the lens of unwavering faith is a testament to who she is. She doesn't just walk the walk; she invites others to walk with her, hand-in-hand with Jesus.

To read this book is to step into the presence of the Holy Spirit. You'll feel it. You'll know it. And you'll leave these pages changed.

Whether you're in a season of struggle or strength, of healing or hope, this book will meet you where you are. And through it all, it will gently guide you back to the One who carries every burden and casts out every fear, Jesus.

Carmen, thank you for your obedience to God's call. Thank you for being a vessel of light and love. And thank you for creating a work that will inspire generations to come.

With honor and love,
Hanna Olivas
CEO
She Rises Studios

FOREWORD

By Erica Elliot

In a world often overshadowed by darkness, *Courageous Woman: Casting Cares Upon Jesus* serves as a beacon of hope and inspiration. This remarkable work invites readers into the lives of women who have faced unimaginable trials, emerging not just as survivors but as triumphant warriors of faith.

Carmen Maendel's captivating storytelling weaves together personal narratives and the profound experiences of extraordinary women, showcasing the transformative power of God's love and grace. Each page provides a testament to the resilience of the human spirit anchored in faith, with scriptures that remind us of God's promises.

As a counselor with 30 years of experience in Christian counseling, I believe this book has the potential to help those struggling with life's challenges. It encourages readers to return to a spiritual place, allowing God to guide them. The practical tools and reflection questions within these pages are invaluable for those feeling stuck, guiding them back to God and His Biblical promises.

Having had the privilege of hearing Carmen speak, I can attest to her exuberance, confidence, and deep integrity. Grounded in Godly wisdom, she consistently brings people back to Jesus, reminding us that we are never alone in our struggles.

As you journey through these pages, you will discover insights that illuminate the path to healing and empowerment. From navigating health and relationships to pursuing entrepreneurship, Carmen offers wisdom that resonates with anyone seeking to deepen their connection with God.

This book is not just a collection of stories; it is a guide encouraging us to embrace our divine purpose. Each account is beautifully crafted, drawing you in and leading you back to the heart of God's promises.

May you find inspiration and renewed courage to face your challenges as you read. With God's help, we can rise above our circumstances and walk boldly in our faith.

By Erica Elliott, MS, LPC
Owner of WarriorHeart Healing Hearts, LLC

SUMMARY

This book can be summarized in the following way: This is a book that encapsulates the miraculous and wonderful ways that Jesus Christ works in all of our lives. It highlights my life stories and those of the women who were kind enough to interview with me and share their own personal experiences they had with Jesus Christ. This is a beautiful collection of stories that will take you on a range of emotions as you join the journey of each of these courageous women of God. You will see how God takes something that was bad or negative and transforms it into something positive for His glory. These stories are true, raw, emotional, and incredible examples of ways that God guides and directs each of our lives.

Proverbs 16:9

"A man's heart plans his way, but the LORD directs his steps."

TABLE OF CONTENTS

INTRODUCTION

I would like to be completely honest and transparent with you. I have always dreamed of becoming an author. It has been on my bucket list for a very long time. Did I ever think I would have the opportunity to bring this dream to fruition? That would be a resounding "no." God has opened doors for me this past summer to fall of 2024 in the area of authorship that I never dreamed possible with She Rises Studios and Fenix TV. I feel tremendously blessed to be able to share these windows into my soul through my stories I share with you in this book. I am very excited that there are several women who are willing to openly and transparently share their own experiences they had with God working miraculously in their lives as well.

This is a beautiful collection of stories that will take you on a range of emotions as you join the journey of each of these courageous women of God. You will see how God takes something that was bad or negative and transforms it into something positive for His glory. These stories are true, raw, emotional, and incredible examples of ways that God guides and directs each of our lives. Proverbs 16:9, "A man's heart plans his way, but the LORD directs his steps."

I suggest you get comfortable and snuggle up with your favorite choice of hot beverage to read these incredible stories and testaments of God's goodness and faithfulness in our lives. There will be moments that you laugh, cry, cheer on, and empathize with the women sharing these stories from the depths of their hearts and souls.

I hope and pray that you can read each of these stories and be immensely blessed by them. I also hope you can utilize the additional resources and references provided in this book to help you achieve the best version of yourself.

Wishing you the very best in all your future endeavors.

Let your beautiful journey begin...

Carmen K. Maendel

THESIS STATEMENT: The Common Thread is Faith

It is more favorable to live as a believer in Jesus Christ with the Holy Spirit guiding you along your life than without Him.

My sole purpose for writing this book is to honor and bring glory to God.

The reason I chose "Courageous Woman: Casting Cares Upon Jesus" as the title for my book is because of the definition of the words *casting cares*. Casting cares is the act of giving your worries and anxieties to someone else, such as God, instead of holding onto them. This phrase is based on 1 Peter 5:7, which says, "Casting all your cares on Him, because He cares about you."

CHAPTER 1

MOMENTS OF IMPACT
(MILESTONES)

Introduction: My Identity in Christ

I am Carmen Maendel and I am a child of God. God has blessed me with an incredible husband and son, to travel through life with. Heaven is our true home, and we are just passing through. Everything belongs to God, always has, and always will. I want to preface that any accomplishments or accolades that have happened to me came from God, not me. Everything I do, I do for the glory of God. "I can do all things in Christ who strengthens me" (Philippians 4:13).

I graduated from several colleges and universities with degrees that have helped me honor God in a variety of different ways over the years. I am sharing these details so that as you progress through my narrative, you can see how God used all these life experiences I had to His Glory. My first and only love is Jesus, and everything else stems from there. I am incredibly thankful to have the husband and son I do today. I feel very well grounded in my identity in Christ and have a handful of very close friends I do life with. We have an incredible and supportive church family as well. I married into an amazing God fearing family and inherited many wonderful relatives in the process. My mother and stepmother have also always been there to help guide me along the way. My father and father-in-law passed away in 2009 and 2021, respectively; however, prior to that, they both have also been an incredible beacon to my life.

Formative Years: Glass Shatters & God Shows Up

My story begins with being born and raised in a very influential family. Through God's grace, I discover that my family inheritance pales insurmountably to the inheritance I have waiting for me in Heaven. As I have gotten older, God has revealed to me that money is simply a vehicle used to bless others and for our immediate needs; it is not a means to an end. Family memories are much more precious and valuable than money ever was. I grew up with two siblings older than me, my brother and sister. I remember racing my sister to our dad's lap after dinner while my brother watched and grinned. Lots of competition in our home, some healthy and some not so much. I remember being asked a number of times, "Why can't you be more like your sister?" Today, I am confident in the woman God has created me to be, flaws and all. My mother has been a tremendous influence in my life in a number of different ways. She reminded me about a specific childhood incident that will become a repetitive analogy to the narrative I share with you in the pages to come.

Our family was in the process of adding several additions to our home, and there was a large storm glass window that was propped up against our home. I was playing and somehow that large window fell over the top of my head, causing shards of glass to poke into me on all sides. My mother screamed, "Don't move!" and miraculously, I walked away from that without a single scratch. So, back to my analogy, of my life and this large glass window. Just the same way as the window slammed to the ground and shattered into many pieces, there are moments that life could have fallen and shattered. I look at the moments of impact in my life and how God has used them to completely transform the situation and me to His glory. This has happened a number of times, and God has always faithfully shown up and orchestrated the mini miracles in my life. My life verse is Proverbs 3:5-6, "Trust in the Lord with all your heart and lean not on your own understanding. Acknowledge Him in all ways and He will direct your path." Our family verse today is part of Isaiah 40:31, "They that wait upon the Lord shall renew their strength, they shall mount up with wings as eagles." These two verses have been extremely prevalent in my life, and I have called upon them time after time to solidify my faith in Jesus over and over again.

Middle Stages of Adolescence: Overcoming Parents' Divorce & Salvation

It was during eighth grade that my parents decided that they were no longer compatible with one another, and they got divorced. I always thought my parents would be together forever. I remember how painful this portion of my life was, and how lost I felt as one parent would switch out weekends of being at our home with the other. There were different sets of rules for each parent and massive confusion with consistency and stability at that time of my life. God was present and with me before I even understood who He was. At some of those lowest times in my life, I felt a calming peace about the situation, and knew everything was going to be alright. I remember going to this FCA Fellowship of Christian Athletes retreat, and I received salvation in Jesus Christ for the first time in my life. I felt an overwhelming sense of peace all over my body upon salvation, and this brought me to tears. I call them my happy and relieved tears. A huge weight was removed and replaced by a tranquil sense of peace and serenity. The window had come down and shattered, and yet God picked up the pieces and helped me get through that time of extreme sadness and confusion. Through deep prayer and writing poetry, God helped me work through the pervasive feelings of sadness and loneliness at that time in my life. Things slowly seemed to get better, and I learned to start drawing upon God's strength and not my own.

College Years: Two Major Events God Used to Shape My Life

I had always thought I would get married directly out of high school; however, once again, God had a different plan for my life. Sometimes, unanswered prayers can be blessings in disguise, as it was in my case. I went directly to college after high school, and there I remained for several years and earned degrees in various areas of study. I worked a variety of different jobs, from a jewelry store, retail store, RA in my apartment complex, an oriental rug boutique, and an assistant director at an art gallery. I worked three full-time jobs while carrying a full load of classes for my Speech and Language Pathology undergraduate program at UW-Madison. As I reflect back on that time in my life, I was clearly operating on God's strength and not my own. I feel it is important to share two major events that happened while I was still at Cornell College studying art and business. Once again, that glass window came crashing down, and God was in the middle of my healing and growing my faith. I remember sitting by her bedside with her mother and praying fervently in prayer for her recovery that summer. I remember the call with the bad news like it was yesterday; the trip I almost went on with them. My best friend had possibly fallen asleep at the wheel and crossed the centerline, while coming in direct contact with a truck head-on. Her little brother and his fiancée were killed instantly, and she would miraculously come out of her coma with a head injury. I remember how God worked in our lives that summer of 1992. We would visit her each day, hoping to hear about some improvement in her condition. One day, we were even told to prepare ourselves for the worst; however, God had another plan for her life. She did come out of her coma at the end of the summer, and I will always remember how God orchestrated all those events in only a way He could.

The other very impactful event that happened while I was still in college was that my father was fighting his uphill battle with cancer. He would share his PSA count until it became apparent that the cancer had metastasized to the bone level. The analogy was that of someone throwing many seeds into a field, and the seeds just began growing exponentially. Broken pieces of glass once again, and God was preparing my heart for my dad to pass away. I was devastated when my father went unresponsive, and it was clear he was near the end. I prayed for my dad's salvation as he got closer to the end of his life. I also prayed that he would finally be at peace without all the pain cancer had caused him for several years now. I remember making a pledge to myself that I would get in the very best physical shape that I could and remain there. Cancer ran on my dad's side, and strokes and diabetes on my mom's, so I figured I'd better get in top physical shape in case something ever happened to me. Thus, the idea for Maendel Fitness was conceived, and God brought it to fruition for the next eight years. I am very passionate about health and fitness and delighted in sharing everything I learned in these areas with my clients. I formed very tight relationships with them and helped them break through barriers they did not even know they had, using God's strength and not their own.

I do not want to get ahead of myself, though. I continued to work at various positions while I was still in school and even after I finished my program at UW-Madison in Speech and Language Pathology. I saw God show up repetitively in my life, a number of times, when I knew I was not making wise decisions about my life. I had a failed first marriage and made foolish decisions in relationships thereafter. Even then, I felt God prompting me away from my poor lifestyle choices toward his safe haven. He always gave me an out in every situation possible, and usually I was obedient to take it. I know He was putting a hedge of protection over me and had His hand on my life, even before I understood what it means to have a personal relationship with Jesus Christ to the depth that I do today.

Working in Corporate America: Heading Toward Wealth & Rededication to Jesus Christ

So, this brings me to the period of life when I worked as a Special Education Teacher down south while I was still married to my first husband. I loved teaching and felt very privileged to make a difference in these children's lives. I taught middle school for a couple of years and then made the switch to high school upon our move out west. I continued to get one-year teaching contracts and would be forced to move to another position the following year, as I was one of the youngest teachers a board, and the others already had tenure at that time. When enrollment dropped, so would my contract. Once again, shattered broken glass; however, God showed up loud and clear. I prayed about the continuation of teaching Special Education or branching out to something new. God brought an answer to that prayer through one of the parents of my high school students. One of the parents of the young man I taught math to was the Executive Director of the Edward D. Jones investment firm. She asked me if I had ever considered becoming a stockbroker and financial advisor. I taught English and Math, so it seemed to be a pretty sensible progression toward that field. After several panel interviews, passing the Series 7 Stockbroker exam, and acceptance to the company, I was well on my way to the top. I was starting new after my divorce with a new career, a new place to live, and a new car, my JAG. My father was an orthopedic surgeon and became very wealthy by age forty, and I was heading in that same direction myself. The focus was more accounts and more money, and the higher I moved up on that corporate ladder. Instead of shards of glass coming this time, my husband offered knowledge that would help me grow closer to God. God was using my husband as a conduit to help pull me away from the love of money and materialism and closer to Him. I remember when he would come and frequent the bank I worked at on a regular basis. We had an incredible friendship that eventually grew into love and marriage down the road. Both of us had been in failed marriages the first time, and we wanted to move slowly and tread carefully. My husband was instrumental in leading me to Christ as a full-grown woman. There were also two other close friends at the time who helped with that process, Mariana and Shari. On November 4, 2006, I rededicated my life to Jesus Christ while Mariana held my hands and prayed with me. I once again felt the heaviness lifted away from me, which was replaced with warmth and peace. It was a cold evening that night. I remember feeling like a warm blanket was enveloping my body.

Married Life Years: Drawing Closer to My Savior, Jesus Christ

My husband would lure me away from the nightclubs by standing in the doorway while I was on the dance floor. I saw something in my husband that was so pure and beautiful, and I wanted that for myself. The very attractive quality that I saw permeate my husband's whole being was Jesus Christ in him. The bar had less of a pull on me, as my appetite was growing for this new, attractive quality about my husband that I had never experienced before. It was the opposite of confusion and chaos, and it was a feeling of purity and overwhelming peace that drew me in. He also changed the automatic music settings in my JAG to Christian music. I began to like the Christian music and the feeling I got when I listened to it in my car. We began to attend church and Bible study outside of church together. I remember a turning point in my life where I was confronted with a decision: 1) go downtown and party with my colleagues from working at the bank, or 2) go to church to meet up with my future husband that night. I obviously chose the latter of the two choices, and my life progressively began to improve on all levels. I left my position at the bank and spent more time with my future husband and his friends. Later, I found out that my husband's friends had been praying that I would come into his life without even knowing who I was at that time.

My husband and I had a sweet friendship and were the best of friends for an entire year prior to any romantic involvement with one another. God shielded us both from focusing on a physical attraction to one another and instead helped us form a lifelong bond of emotional attraction. Today, we still comment on how happy we are that we did not rush into things and took that year to get to know one another. He asked my dad and stepmom for their blessing for my hand in marriage. He planted daffodils in the shape of a heart with them on the day he asked for my hand in marriage. We were engaged in March of 2007 and married that July, with a very short length of engagement. A couple of years later and our son was born. Glass came flying at us once again, as he was an emergency C-section birth with the cord wrapped very tightly around his neck. God showed up and gave us the strength: "Trust in the Lord with all your heart and lean not on your own understanding. Acknowledge Him in all ways and He will direct your path" (Proverbs 3:5-6). We all needed to get through this complicated birth. Our family verse, Isaiah 40:31, was painted on the nursery wall of his

room and also showed up in the chapel of the hospital where he was born. Coincidence or not? I think not. This was all God! We later had the same artist create a mobile replica of the same eagle painting with Isaiah 40:31 on a painting we have hanging in our living room today. Also, when we had him dedicated and gave him a plaque, the same dedication verse Joshua 1:9, "Have I not commanded you? Be strong and courageous. Do not be afraid; do not be discouraged, for the Lord your God will be with you wherever you go," was found on the wall of the room he was dedicated to. Confirmation!

Several times, we started to make a move back to where I grew up, and God intervened. The home we almost purchased in my hometown was flooded a year later. The same thing happened when we tried to move to a home in the area where we live now. Scattered glass and God were putting it back together. Both times, the sales fell through at the last minute, and it was a blessing in disguise. We almost moved to the cities, and after our near encounter with a drug lord, we decided that was not where we wanted to raise our family. God revealed the plan to us to have us live in the home we have now, with five acres, to accommodate our company we have today.

Married Life Years: What You Will Never Be Prepared to Have Happen in Life

We need to revert to our lives after our son was born and see possibly the greatest area God has impacted my life at a deep emotional time of sorrow. We had gotten the news that we were pregnant again. A few short weeks earlier, I remember a trip to the state fair with a close friend, Traci. She did not understand why I was eating everything under the sun at the fair, and neither did I at that time. Shortly after that trip to the fair, we received the incredible news that we were pregnant again. We celebrated and were absolutely elated when we found out it was twins! Two heartbeats, not one. I remember hitting my knees and calling out to God, "Thank you so much for this incredible blessing of twins in our lives." Twins run on my husband's side of the family, and no one has had twins yet in the family. His mom was a twin. We were super excited and started to mentally, spiritually, and physically plan for the arrival of these two precious bundles of joy into our lives. We began to plan for more space in our home and made the necessary accommodations for their arrival. Broken glass hurled at us at an exorbitant speed, hitting with the news that our doctor could no longer detect any heartbeat inside me. We were absolutely crushed, and it would require God's healing hand to help me emerge from my deep pit of despair and instant depression. I fell to my knees once again, "God, why, why would you give these two beautiful children to us only to have them snatched from our hands?" This started the lifelong process of healing my heart, mourning broken dreams, and just getting my head above water again. A little over a year later, we lost another baby at the exact same time, six weeks and two days into the pregnancy. Healing and encouraging scriptures in the Bible, in the Psalms, were particularly comforting then and continue to be so today. At one point, I made the decision that I could either be sad about losing our babies or glad for the gift of our son we already had. I could become bitter about this scenario in life, or I could become better and let God heal me over a course of time. I opted for the latter on both accounts.

Married Life Years: Exploring An Alternative to Expand Our Family

Adoption was something we would start to explore over the next few years. My husband and I got certified and ready to accept a child or even a children's group into our family. We were preparing our hearts and letting God do the rest. We read books and watched hours of videos about adopting young children into our home. Our son was super excited as well, as he had always wished for a sibling or siblings to join our family. We were ready to start the process of fostering to adopt. Broken glass showed up again in our lives during the process of attempting to adopt children into our family. "They that wait upon the Lord shall renew their strength, they shall mount up with wings as eagles" (Isaiah 40:31). Timing seemed to be our biggest hurdle, as the adoption agency only had children for us at inopportune times in our lives. We tried one other time later as well, and broken glass guided us back to the struggles our son was having at that time. After heavy prayer, we decided it may not be the best time to introduce more children into our family equation.

Married Life Years: Traveling the World & New Business Dreams

Over the next few years, my husband and I did a lot of traveling abroad. We went to Mexico several times, once with our son even, and Italy to celebrate ten years of marriage together. We enjoyed the freedom of not having young children in our home, and occasionally offered to watch our friend's children to help fill that deep void inside. Broken glass shattered, in the form of adoption, was soon to be replaced with other dreams God had for us. God was saying no to one dream, and was about to introduce us to a whole other set of dreams for us and our family. As our son was in school, I began to pray about ways I could invest my time wisely during the day. This is how the idea came about to start a company, with a close friend of mine, Traci Galles, which became Genoa Denim and Leather Apparel. We bought designer jeans and purses wholesale and sold them at retail. We traveled around the state and set up trade shows to introduce our merchandise to the community. At the end of the year, we sold the company for a profit.

I have always had a passion for photography, and I enjoy taking pictures of a variety of different topics and subjects. After heavy prayer, I felt led to launch Carmen Maendel Photography the following year. I was able to capture photographs of families, birthday parties, graduations, and, of course, wildlife and sell them. I started placing my photographs on various platforms to see how they would perform with other fellow photographers around the world. The piece that has received the most attention in worldwide contests and has placed in the top ten percent of the world is called "A Little Loony." This piece was taken when we were out on our boat, and a family of loons was close to us on the water. The father and mother loon did not dive deep because their baby could not dive, and remained on the surface of the water. They did the same, and as we crept closer to them, the father loon put his wings out and leaned toward me and my camera. The light was perfect to pick up the vivid reflection on the water. God blessed me with the perfect timing of that shot!

New Business Dreams: Overcoming Fear in My Life Through Jesus Christ

Reflecting back on my father's passing, God led me to start a ministry with health and fitness, which eventually became Maendel Fitness. When we first moved to this home, I decided to set up a mini gym in the basement. I felt selfish and convicted just using it myself, so I started inviting my friends to come work out with me in the gym. I realized how much of a blessing it could be for many ladies at once, and I started a health and fitness ministry in my church. For four years, about five to six ladies came consistently to work out in the gym with me. We even had an area designated for their small children directly connected to the gym. I loved it so much that I decided to pursue my Certified Fitness Trainer license and opened Maendel Fitness officially in 2016. I later added my Master's in Nutrition and Precision Nutrition, followed by DNA Testing and Analysis. There were many lessons learned, and I overcame a variety of different fears embarking on this adventure from 2016 to 2023. My biggest fear was the fear of live video. I came to the realization that I did not have to be perfect. I could be "perfectly imperfect" or even "flawsome"! I could be full of flaws and awesome at the same time. I am created in God's image, and I am beautiful in His sight as a perfect image bearer of Christ. Jesus is the only one who is perfect, so I learned that I should not fear being less than perfect on live video. This was very freeing and allows me to be authentically me in front of the camera now. I have learned to improvise and work with ad-lib situations, and half the time, I realize that I am the only one who would view something as a mistake on camera. Others may not even detect that mistake at all.

This realization has allowed me to go way outside my comfort zone and crush different fears and obstacles that used to stand in my way! God blessed me with a YouTube channel with workout videos and health and fitness information that I created. I created this with God's strength, not my own. I worked with two mentors and coaches who helped me break through barriers and accomplish business goals: James Allen and Mercile Martinsen. I am very thankful for their wisdom and guidance. They both helped me push through some of my own fears that would have prevented me from helping my clients crush their own fears, limitations, or suppositions. One of the ways God showed me to help my clients overcome their fears was by having them pick a Bible verse that they can stand by and identify with as their life verse. He also showed me how to help them identify and record "I Can" statements on paper to increase their level of confidence in themselves. One final way God led me to help them is by using my **MFC Confidence Boost System:**

"Getting Rid of Insecurities, Negative Thoughts, and Negative Beliefs"

1. Learn to Shift Your Negative Thoughts
2. Push Your Negative Thought Out
3. Question the Belief
4. Create a Negative Association with This Old Belief
5. Create a Positive Association with the New Belief

My clients used this system when they were trying to get rid of negative beliefs and thought patterns about themselves. This system did just that.

God also guided me in creating and implementing the MFC Muscle Menu into my business, which taught and allowed my clients to pick and choose various exercises they would perform. This was set up similarly to a menu you would find at a restaurant. I divided the body into various subheadings with individual exercises targeting those muscle groups. For example, if one of my clients wanted to work the upper body in their biceps, triceps, and pecs, then they could pick from that menu to create three or four exercises working those muscles and muscle groups. Along with this, God also showed me, through prayer, how to put together a Gym List of the top ten items you would need at the gym. My clients appreciated these additional resources to help them work out independently on their own.

Another tool God helped me create, after heavy prayer, and implement with my clients was my MFC Guru Grocery List. I created a list of foods using the Divine Nine food groups and categorized each under every vitamin and mineral. A person could use this in conjunction with my DNA Testing & Analysis and supplement the areas of vitamins and minerals that they may be deficient in. They would simply need to search for the foods listed on my sheet to help them boost a particular vitamin or mineral. This was very helpful for my clients in guiding and directing them toward healthy eating patterns and shopping for food at the grocery store for their families. In addition to the MFC Guru Grocery List, God also guided me toward the production of an MFC Tasty & Savory Cookbook with several healthy recipes that kept my clients on the right track.

Another fear I faced was the fear of being an imposter. The closer I drew to God and realized my identity in Christ, the less fear I had in this area of my life. It was easier to be the person God created me to be and more of my authentic self than it was to pretend to be someone that I was not for several years. I did several sports and fitness modeling shoots when I first started my company. I thought I had to portray a "perfect image" in order to sell my company. In retrospect, a lot of my clients liked the fact that I was real and not like a Barbie doll. I also came to the conclusion that it was not my company; it belonged to God, not me. I needed to honor God in all I did, including treating my body as a temple of the Holy Spirit. I was convicted in this area of my life, and stopped doing the sports and fitness modeling shoots altogether.

One final fear I addressed while I owned Maendel Fitness was the fear of the unknown. I learned amazing lessons about trusting God and holding on loosely to everything in my life. None of it belongs to me; it all belongs to God. We had to remodel our gym twice due to storm damage, and in the end, did an expensive full waterproofing project just to save our gym and my company. I learned to trust God and have faith in Him. Thus, I had faith in myself. Faith is where there is no evidence or proof, an unshakable faith in God. "Therefore, since we have been justified through faith, we have peace with God through our Lord Jesus Christ, through whom we have gained access by faith into this grace in which we now stand. And we boast in the hope of the glory of God" (Romans 5:1-2). I had peace and trusted the fact that God wanted me to close everything down in the business when my husband was offered a position out of town, and we were forced to put our home on the market for sale. I was obedient and closed everything, including the online program, Rock Hard Body. I did not understand at that time that He was going to ask me to work side by side with my husband in our company today, Nate's Property Maintenance LLC.

New Business Dreams: Husband & Wife Team Owning/Operating Nate's Property Maintenance LLC

Glass shards shooting toward me once again, and I'm calling out to God, "Why?" Why did God bless me with a complete gym, with all the extra amenities, only to have me shut it all down? This is biblical faith in God. He knows better than I do, and He knows my needs and desires better than I do. I see now that we were not supposed to sell our home with five acres on it, because we now use this home and acreage to run our business today. I needed to close one business in order to help run the next one. It makes sense to me now, and God has blessed our current company exponentially since last year on many different levels. God has shown us the most tremendous growth in the last year and a half through our profits, expanding our business inventory, and adding a team of workers to our company.

We are a husband-and-wife team. I handle all business on the home front, and my husband works with our clients and his team of workers on our job sites. One of the strategies God showed me, through prayer, was to use our existing SEO for Maendel Fitness to help raise the SEO for Nate's Property Maintenance LLC quickly by advertising on the same strong social media platforms. I gradually adapted all of them to our new business. It is all about the algorithms when it comes to Google and SEO. After praying with my husband about branding our company, I decided to post before and after pictures regularly on Facebook, Instagram, LinkedIn, Angi, and Alignable, and we have begun to rise towards the top of the Google list. We get the majority of our client leads for our company through referrals of existing clients and organic marketing off the internet. We do very little in paid advertisements, with the exception of our website and marketing through First Hit LLC, for our company at this time. I know God has prepared me for all my business and financial responsibilities in our company's partnership through the past degrees, career positions, and life experiences God has blessed me with. Each day, God shows me how we can be a blessing to those around us, and I am paying close attention. We are blessed in our current company so that we can bless others. I know I can trust God with everything in my life. "'For I know the plans I have for you,' declares the LORD, 'plans to prosper you and not to harm you, plans to give you hope and a future'" (Jeremiah 29:11). I will continue to trust God and be obedient in the areas that He has asked me to serve, and I will not lean on my own understanding in my business and personal life.

The Ultimate Life Lesson: It's Not About Me & It's All About Jesus

The biggest lesson I have learned through the summation of all my life experiences is the following: It is not about me, it is everything about Christ! Whatever I do in life, Christ needs to be in the center, and He gets all the credit, accolades, and glory, not me. A Godly friend of mine pointed me toward these incredibly encouraging verses. I would like to share them with you now, in hopes that they will touch your heart as they have mine: Philippians 3:7-14.

"But whatever were gains to me I now consider loss for the sake of Christ. What is more, I consider everything a loss because of the surpassing worth of knowing Christ Jesus my Lord, for whose sake I have lost all things. I consider them garbage, that I may gain Christ and be found in him, not having a righteousness of my own that comes from the law, but that which is through faith in Christ—the righteousness that comes from God on the basis of faith. I want to know Christ—yes, to know the power of his resurrection and participation in his sufferings, becoming like him in his death, and so, somehow, attaining to the resurrection from the dead. Not that I have already obtained all this, or have already arrived at my goal, but I press on to take hold of that for which Christ Jesus took hold of me. Brothers and sisters, I do not consider myself to have taken hold of it yet. But one thing I do: Forgetting what is behind and straining toward what is ahead, I press on toward the goal to win the prize for which God has called me heavenward in Christ Jesus."

The Gospel: The Good News

"For those of you who don't know the joy of serving the Lord Jesus Christ or the peace that comes from His forgiveness, I'd like to introduce you to my Savior..."

The word Gospel means "good news." It's pretty important to understand that. The Bible is not a book that tells us what we have to do to earn salvation; it is a book that tells us what God did to earn our salvation. What He did was send Jesus. Jesus did for us what we could never do for ourselves, and He paid for what we had done in His body on the cross. God created human beings and intended for them to be ruling creatures. We were supposed to be under God but over everything else. We were supposed to rule over creation under the guidance and authority of God's Word and to function as conduits for all the blessings of heaven. That's how it was supposed to be, but unfortunately, the Bible tells the story of how our first parents, Adam and Eve, fell into sin by choosing to rebel against God's Word by being tricked by Satan to eat from the tree of Knowledge of Good and Evil. From that point on, humanity has been on a downward spiral, moving further and further away from God and our original design and glory. The heart of the Gospel is the Good News that Jesus has come as God in the flesh and has obeyed God perfectly and has therefore obtained the right to all the blessings God originally intended to give to men and women.

Furthermore, through his sacrificial death on the cross, He has paid the debt that we owed to God for disobeying his commands. There is therefore no need anymore for us to hide from God. In Jesus, we can come home, and we can be restored through His forgiveness and repentance of our sins. We not only get the gift of Eternal Life, but we also get the honor and privilege of having a personal relationship with Jesus after accepting Him into our hearts. We praise Him, worship Him, and come to Him in prayer daily. We were created with the sole purpose of honoring and glorifying God through all of our thoughts, actions, and verbal utterances. The climax of the Gospel is the great news that He rose from the dead and ascended into heaven, where he now intercedes on our behalf. He gives the Holy Spirit to all his people, and he slowly but surely changes our hearts, reforms our desires, and teaches us how to be the children of God we were always intended to be. For now, Jesus remains in heaven, changing the world one person at a time, but one day He will return and judge the world in righteousness. He will remove from this world all sin and all causes of sin, and He will restore all to a state of peace, prosperity, and flourishing, and all those who have received Him as their Lord and Savior will participate in His rule and enjoy His goodness forever.

Please refer to John in the Bible for further explanation of the Gospel.

Lessons & Reflection

1. What adversity am I facing in my life right now?
2. How do I trust God while I am discovering my true identity in Christ?
3. Has adversity drawn me closer to God or pushed me away from Him?
4. What is my biggest life obstacle, and how did I overcome it?
5. How do I get out of struggling with adversity?

_____

_____

_____

_____

_____

_____

_____

_____

_____

_____

_____

_____

_____

CHAPTER 2

DAUGHTER OF OUR MOST HIGH KING
(COMPASS)

Introduction: My Identity in Jesus Christ

Have you ever asked yourself: W*hat is my identity, and where is my identity derived from?* I am Carmen Maendel and I am a child of God! My identity lies in Christ alone! My desire is that God will speak through me to share my life experiences with you and encourage you to seek your own identity in Christ. I have shared in detail in my chapter "Moments of Impact" in this book, if you would like to refer to that as a solid foundation for this chapter, "Daughter of Our Most High King." On November 4th, 2006, I rededicated my life to Jesus Christ after coming to Him first at the very young age of thirteen. My life meandered in many different directions, and not all the choices and decisions I made were healthy ones at that time in my life or even now. My saving and growing faith is something I choose to work on every day of my life. I will always fall short because Jesus is the only one who is perfect. I have discovered that I can be flaw-some, though, full of flaws and awesome at the same time. My desire is to share with you my spiritual journey of life, how I pray, live, and lead by faith.

I find inspiration in 2 Peter 1:5-10, "But also this very reason, giving all diligence, add to your faith virtue; to virtue, knowledge; to knowledge, self-control; to self-control, perseverance; to perseverance, godliness; and to godliness, brotherly kindness; to brotherly kindness, love. For if these things are yours and abound, you will be neither barren nor unfruitful in the knowledge of our Lord Jesus Christ. For he who lacks these things is shortsighted, even to blindness, and has forgotten that he was cleansed from his old sins. Therefore, brethren, be even more diligent to make your call and election sure, for if you do these things you will never stumble." I also must add discipline to knowledge; moderation about worldly things; and add self-restraint, patience, and joyful submission to the will of God. These are the things I strive for in my Christian walk daily. I know that God has a will for my life, and He knows better what I need and desire than I do myself. It takes the pressure off of me, feeling like I have to be in control of my life every second of every day. Instead, I place my whole faith and belief in God, and that He has my best interest at heart, regardless of whether it lines up with my belief system and deepest desires. God's part is His Sovereignty and Promises to us, and our part is Trust, Faith, and Commitment to Him. Trust + Faith + Commitment = Success! Let's break this verse apart to see how each part of it can help us pray, live, and lead by faith.

Faith + Virtue + Knowledge + Self-Control + Perseverance + Godliness + Brotherly Kindness + Love = The Christian Walk

Faith

"But without faith it is impossible to please Him, for he who comes to God must believe that He is, and is a rewarder of those who diligently seek Him" (Hebrews 1:1-6). The significance of faith in the life of a believer is necessary to both please God and live because we have been justified. Hebrews 10:38, "Now the just shall live by faith; But if anyone draws back, My soul has no pleasure in him." We must know God as He is revealed in the Word, and understand the requirements He has for each of us. As I read and meditate on the Word, my living faith in God produces fruit. This can be very difficult at times to understand why things happen the way they do in life. I remember when my parents got divorced, and I did not understand why this would happen to all of us in life. I did know that God had a plan for our lives, and things would be alright. Faith is believing in the things that we can not see tangibly, directly in front of us. I believe that the difficulties that we encounter can help our faith grow stronger. We can either become bitter or better in a situation, and the choices we make lead us to various outcomes in life. I trust, believe, and have full reliance on God. Hebrews 11:1, "Now faith is the substance of things hoped for, the evidence of things not seen."

Virtue or Goodness

Another way to say goodness is to have varying degrees of moral excellence. I will not achieve full goodness while I'm here on this earth because we live in a fallen world. No one is perfect except Jesus Christ. We can strive to emulate Christ on many different levels; however, we will always fall short on this side of Heaven because we are human and not God. Unless I have a genuine desire and a willingness in my heart to do the right thing in life, all progress will come to a stop. I have free will, and sometimes I feel that battle between my flesh and spirit. One example of this is in the music I choose to listen to. I love everything about the country and was raised in the country. I enjoy country hats, boots, music, and the laid-back atmosphere that it provides. If I am honest with myself, though, some of the country music I listen to doesn't feed my spirit, and it does feed my flesh. These are daily decisions I need to make in order to live a life that is full of prayer, worship, and adoration for my Lord, Jesus Christ. If I am not drawing closer to

Christ, then I am moving away from Him. In the same token, I am always worshiping something, and if it is not Christ-centered, it is worldly and probably not feeding my spirit within. Philippians 4:8, "Finally, brethren, whatsoever things are true, whatsoever things are honest, whatsoever things are just, whatsoever things are pure, whatsoever things are lovely, whatsoever things are of good report; if there be any virtue, and if there be any praise, think on these things."

Virtues in Life

Brave, Temperate, Generous, Truthful, Witty, Friendly, Spirited, Conscientious, Benevolent, Industrious.

Isn't it amazing that if you look at a variant of these virtues on either the deficiency side or the excess side that they can mean completely different things. An example of this is someone who is Brave and is practicing that virtue in life. However, if they are deficient in being Brave, they are Cowardly, and if they are in excess of being Brave, they are Arrogant. Another example of this is Industrious. The deficiency of Industrious is Lazy, and the excessiveness of Industrious is an Overachiever. Balance is so important in life, and the above examples of being Brave and Industrious point to how important balance truly is to attain in our lives.

Knowledge

Proverbs is a place I go to regularly in the Bible to seek out knowledge about life in general. My life verse is Proverbs 3:5-6, "Trust in the Lord with all your heart and lean not on your own understanding. Acknowledge Him in all ways and He will make your path straight." Many times, I have referred to this verse and been comforted by knowing that God sees things very differently than we do. I can, therefore, "choose not to be offended" in various situations, knowing that God is in complete and utter control, and I may not understand the complete picture of a scenario in life. Our family life verse is Isaiah 40:31, "They that wait upon the Lord shall renew their strength, they shall mount up with wings as eagles, They shall run and not be weary, They shall walk and not faint." There have been numerous times that our family has relied heavily on this verse as God has us in His "waiting room" during that period of our lives. Our attitudes while we are in the "waiting room" are equally important. God has always been faithful in His promises in working things out in our lives in His timing and His way. This may not directly correlate with what we think should happen or when it should happen in our lives. God is working on me in this area of my life to be still and wait and trust that He has everything taken care of and is completely in control of every situation in my life.

I feel it is very important to pursue knowledge about God; however, it is equally important for that knowledge to be able to move into the heart level as well. We need to seek Jesus with our whole hearts. Proverbs 3:13-14 reminds us of the following: "Happy is the man who finds wisdom, and the man who gains understanding: for her proceeds are better than the profits of silver, and her gain more than fine gold." We can't stop here, though; we need to have self-control along with that knowledge. We need some way to put that knowledge into practice.

Self-Control

Having the knowledge to do the right thing is only half of the equation. We need to apply that knowledge to our everyday lives or practice living out the truth that we believe in our hearts about Jesus. Matthew 7:24,

"Therefore whoever hears these sayings of Mine, and does them, I will liken him to a wise man who builds his house on a rock." Having a solid foundation of Christ is like a man who builds his house on a rock instead of sand. Placing healthy boundaries and sticking to them in life is one way I exercise self-control in my life. I do make mistakes in life and let my guard down at times, and that is the small foothold Satan uses to cause havoc in my life. Sometimes, the "little foxes," if not dealt with immediately and snuffed out, can become huge obstacles in our lives. I have learned this lesson the hard way in the past. One area in which I have demonstrated a great deal of self-control is my passionate dedication to fitness and nutrition. I have always had a passion for these two things, and working out and healthy eating are part of my lifestyle. I believe in the 80/20 philosophy when it comes to working out and eating healthy. Eighty percent of the time, I feel you should pay close attention to eating nutritious foods and working out in the gym or the great outdoors. The remaining twenty percent of the time, you should take a break from that by eating what you want in moderation and giving your body a rest from the gym. If you have a problem starting a workout program, it is not because you lack motivation. Instead, it is because you lack discipline. As you practice self-control and stick to it, you move toward perseverance. 2 Timothy 1:7 says, "For God gave us a spirit not of fear but of power and love and self-control." With the Holy Spirit inside of us, we are able to possess self-control and demonstrate the fruits of the Spirit. As a result, we can live in a way that is honorable to God.

Perseverance

As I reflect on the following: **Faith + Goodness + Knowledge + Self-Control**, I realize I am able to discipline myself and work toward perseverance. I will not stop striving to live a life that pleases the Lord, even if I mess up consistently in my walk. This is also where repentance and the request for forgiveness come in. Forgiveness, mercy, and grace interweave throughout my life, allowing me to forgive, ask for forgiveness, and restore broken relationships in my life. I have the perseverance to move through adversity in life, especially in business. God has blessed me with four businesses in the past twelve years for opportunities to develop the fruits of the Spirit: **Love, Joy, Peace, Patience, Kindness, Goodness, Faithfulness, Gentleness, and Self-Control.** I remember when my husband and I had just met, and I presented my list of Seventy Non-Negotiable items to him. We laugh about it now; however, we went through every item on that list created before I was a child of God, and Nate presented the Fruits of the Spirit to me. He told me that those were the things he was looking for in a Godly wife. One example that I had to exercise faith and patience in the Lord was when we had extreme storm damage to our gym. We remodeled the gym twice, and the third time we underwent a very expensive waterproofing system in order to keep my company, Maendel Fitness, open and thriving. I remember standing in water in our basement gym, hand in hand with a dear friend, with tears streaming down my face. At that time, everything seemed hopeless, and it was amazing how a gift of a bucket of KFC chicken could help raise our spirits and increase our faith in God's plan for our gym. We persevered through the process of having drain tile installed around the perimeter and through the center of the gym. We also had a triple-safe sump pump installed in the basement to save our gym. I have learned to work through adversity in business and turn stumbling blocks into stepping stones over the years I have spent owning and operating businesses of my own. When faced with a problem today in our company, I like to be solution-oriented and look at every challenge as a hidden opportunity. What successful situation comes out of any discipline in life without endurance and perseverance? As I strive for perseverance, I move closer toward Godliness. Romans 5:3-4, "Not only so, but we also rejoice in our sufferings, because we know that suffering produces perseverance; perseverance, character; and character, hope." Romans 2:6-7, "Who will render to each one according to his deeds eternal life to those who by patient continuance in doing good seek for glory, honor, and immortality."

Godliness

We are called in this life to not just persevere through it but to embrace adversity and challenges with a Godly view, striving as much as we can toward Godliness. "That you may work worthy of the Lord, fully pleasing Him, being fruitful in every good work and increasing in the knowledge of God" (Colossians 1:10). We need to train ourselves with perseverance so we have the endurance to push ourselves toward Godliness. God shows us the example we are to live by, by reaching out to us with His love, and we need to reach out to others by living a Godly life. The Commandments point toward the idea of us first and foremost loving our God with all our heart, and secondly, loving our neighbor. We can not love others if we do not love God first. I pray every day for God to help me emulate Him and be more like Him in every way, shape, and form. I also pray that I can be a blessing to others. I believe that God blesses us so that we can bless others. We have been tremendously blessed with our company, Nate's Property Maintenance LLC, today, which has led to the opportunity to bless others by pouring into their lives. As Nate and I lead our company, we aim to serve our clientele and build deeper relationships with them. Even though I know I fall short, I will continue to better myself in all areas, striving toward Godliness, pleasing our Lord, and moving toward Brotherly Kindness. 1 Timothy 6:6-8, "But godliness with contentment is great gain, for we brought nothing into the world, and we cannot take anything out of the world."

Brotherly Kindness

When there is a fire in our hearts, and we look outwardly instead of inwardly to ourselves, we begin to move toward Brotherly Kindness. As we focus more on God first and then others, we take the focus off of us and place it on other people. We begin to show compassion and empathy toward others by placing ourselves in their shoes. When we love God first, it gives us the ability to reach out in love to others. **Faith + Virtue + Knowledge + Self-Control + Perseverance + Godliness = Brotherly Kindness.** When you look at all of these combined together, it leads you to Brotherly Kindness and Love. I had the opportunity to practice all of these as I worked with and trained ladies in our gym for eight years. I remember being able to meet my clients right where they were at and help encourage them in their fitness journeys along the way, placing God in the center of my business. I remember laughing, crying, and everything in between as I helped guide them along as God guided me to do so. One thing I had my clients do was to choose a memory verse from the Bible that would help encourage them and relate to God on a very personal level. I wish I had done this at the very beginning of launching my company in 2016. I realized as I trained my clients over the years how important the spiritual mind and body connection was, and I dove more into that in the last half of the eight years I was training ladies in our gym. The Golden Rule is always a good place to start with Brotherly Kindness, also known as the ethic of reciprocity, meaning that we should reciprocate to others how we would like to be treated ourselves. Matthew 7:12, "So in everything, do to others what you would have them do to you, for this sums up the Law and the Prophets." I remember that as I was training women in our gym, I never asked them to do or perform an exercise or task that I was not willing to do myself. I would push them to challenge themselves through various tasks and barriers; however, I also knew that everyone has their own limit of capacity. I tried to be sensitive to those limits, and build my clients up for success and not failure due to my own "unrealistic" expectations of them. Brotherly Kindness brings us full circle back to love. God loves us so much that He gave His only son to die in place of our sins so that we could have eternal life and the gift of the Holy Spirit living inside of us! "For God so loved the world that He gave His only begotten Son, that whoever believes in Him should not perish but have everlasting life" (John 3:16).

Love

Faith + Virtue + Knowledge + Self-Control + Perseverance + Godliness + Brotherly Kindness + Love = The Christian Walk. As I move through my life journey and concentrate on each and every one of the above things, I am reminded that in order to love others and do all these things, I must wholly and completely love God first. I will continue to pray while I am in the gym on my tread climber daily, pray before each meal, pray throughout the day, pray when I have lost something and can't find it, pray when a friend reaches out to me, pray for my family members and friends, pray with my church family, pray at nighttime during family devotions and bedtime. The ultimate level of love God shows us is revealed in John 3:16, and the ultimate level of love we can show others is to pray for them. God commands us to pray even for our enemies. The funny thing is that when you start to really pray for someone that you consider your enemy, the feelings of dislike soon dissipate as you bathe them in prayer. Praying and loving our enemies is one form of being obedient to God and His will for our lives. Try it sometime; pray for someone who may rub you the wrong way and truly try to understand life in their shoes, and you will find that you may not carry so much disdain for that person as you thought you did. Love covers all sin, "And above all things have fervent love for one another, for love will cover a multitude of sins" (1 Peter 4:8).

When my husband and I got married, our pastor read 1 Corinthians 13:4-8, "Love is patient, love is kind. It does not envy, it does not boast, it is not proud. It does not dishonor others, it is not self-seeking, it is not easily angered, and it keeps no record of wrongs. Love does not delight in evil but rejoices with the truth. It always protects, always trusts, always hopes, always perseveres." It is difficult for me to fathom how much God loves me and all of you. I frequently go back to this verse to break apart the different characteristics of what love is and what it is not.

The Christian Walk

Galatians 5:16, "But I say, walk by the Spirit, and you will not gratify the desires of the flesh." So, if we apply to our lives the combination of all of the above—Faith, Virtue, Knowledge, Self-Control, Perseverance, Godliness, Brotherly Kindness, and Love—we achieve the Christian Walk. What does this tangibly look like? The Christian Walk is a spiritual gift and blessing of God's grace. We are saved by grace through faith in Jesus Christ. As believers, we are the chosen children of God. We have fellowship with God through Jesus, and we have fellowship with other believers as well. As Christians, we serve God and have a servant's heart toward others. As we learn more about Jesus, we are able to apply that knowledge to our everyday lives. Spiritual battles come readily as we live in a fallen world, and there are always the forces of good and evil around us. God has commanded us to go out and share the Good News of the gospel with everyone we meet and know. Finally, our Christian Walk is a spiritual devotion to God every single day of our lives. We need to keep our lamps ready and waiting for His return, whenever that may be. This is how I want to Pray, Live, and Lead by Faith in my own Christian Walk with God. There are some practical ways I strive to accomplish this using my online program I created in 2022, "Rock Hard Body: Power, Strength, & Fitness." I will share four parts of this with you in the next section of my chapter.

Discovering Your Spiritual Side

The Word is one of the best places we can go to get to know our Heavenly Father. He will help guide our lives, resist temptation, and strengthen us in our challenges. I like to refer to The Parable of the Friend at Midnight. "Never Give-Up Story" Luke 11:5-10, "So I say to you: Ask and it will be given to you; seek and you will find; knock and the door will be opened to you. For everyone who asks receives; the one who seeks finds; and to the one who knocks, the door will be opened." What can be learned from this story? The following things can be derived from this story: appeal to our Father in Heaven, stay focused and be persistent in prayer, have complete faith that He will do more than we ask for, and have faith over fear. If we are reaching out on a daily basis to God in prayer and asking Him for wisdom about the direction of our lives, and have complete faith that He will do even more than we ask for, we have faith over our fears that we are headed in the correct direction. "So Jesus said to them, 'Because of your unbelief, for assuredly, I say to you, if you have faith as a mustard seed, you will say to this mountain, 'Move from here to there,' and it will move; and nothing will be impossible for you'" (Matthew 17:20).

I encouraged my online fitness and nutrition clients to engage in seven pieces of scripture: 1) Luke 18:27, "Jesus replied, 'What is impossible with man is possible with God.'" 2) Matthew 7:7, "Ask and it will be given to you; seek and you will find; knock and the door will be opened to you." 3) 1 Corinthians 2:9, "However, as it is written: 'What no eye has seen, what no ear has heard, and what no human mind has conceived' the things God has prepared for those who love him." 4) Mark 11:23, "Truly I tell you, if anyone says to this mountain, 'Go, throw yourself into the sea,' and does not doubt in their heartbeat believes that what they say will happen, it will be done for them." 5) Ephesians 4:23, "And be renewed in the spirit of our mind." 6) Psalm 51:10, "Create in me a pure heart, O God, and renew a steadfast spirit within me." and 7) Proverbs 3:5-6, "Trust in the Lord with all your heart, And lean not on your own understanding; In all your ways acknowledge Him, And He shall direct your paths." God can do the impossible, and solutions happen according to His will. Expect good things from God and believe that prayer is answered. Be free from all doubt and fear, and allow God to restore our strength to us. Finally, lean not on your own understanding because God has a much bigger and better plan for your life than you can ever contemplate or imagine! I asked my clients to please read, meditate on the above scriptures and try to figure out how each one applies to their lives. I encourage you to do the same right now.

Finally, there is an inspirational story about a donkey falling into a well that I would like to share with you. So, one day the farmer looked around and called out to his donkey, but he was nowhere to be found. As he made his rounds around the farm, he stopped at the well. He heard a faint donkey cry coming from deep within the well. The farmer cried out, "Don't worry, donkey, I will rescue you!" As he started to think of ways to get his friend from the well, the neighbors all gathered around as well. They tried several different ways and eventually gave up. The farmer and the neighbors sadly started to throw dirt into the well to put their dear friend to rest. Each shovel of dirt was thrown as the farmer and neighbors wept. What they did not realize is that every layer of dirt thrown on the donkey, he would shake it off and take a step up. He kept doing this for hours and eventually shook off the last dirt load and stepped out of the well. You can imagine the astonishment and disbelief the farmer and his friends felt as the donkey trotted safely away from the well. Sometimes, things are not what they seem to be, so take heart and never stop pursuing God and everything He has for you in life!

The Muscle of Prayer

As you work out your body each day, don't forget to work out your paramount muscle of prayer! We had the opportunity through God to pray through a very painful chapter in our lives. My husband and I had gotten the news that we were pregnant again. We were over the moon ecstatic when we found out it was twins. We had already been blessed with our son, Joshua, and we were excited to have more babies join our family unit. We started to make all the necessary preparations to have these two sweet bundles of joy integrate into our lives. We had prayed for more children after having our son, Joshua, and God had blessed us with twins. We continued to go for our routine hospital checkups, and everything seemed to be progressing normally at that time. The next part is very hard to write about and talk about even to this day. I still remember going into the hospital to have our ultrasound done with my husband, and the look on the face of the nurse who could not find two heartbeats anymore. We were in shock and disbelief that this dream we had to expand our family had come to a screeching halt right there and then in the hospital room at six weeks and two days into our pregnancy. We had prayed for more children, and now we needed to pray to release our twins back to God and pray for healing and restoration in our lives. Why do we pray?

We pray because this helps develop our relationship with God. It helps us understand His loving nature, and He helps provide answers to our lives. He helps us find direction in our lives through prayer, and He gives us strength when we need it most. He also gives us strength to avoid temptation by always providing a way out for us in any given situation. God wants us to communicate with Him through prayer, and He always listens to us when we pray. God may not answer our prayer how we want Him to or in the time frame we desire. Why is prayer so important in our lives? Prayer aligns us with God's will for us. Prayer and fasting help us accept God's will for our lives. Prayer can work miracles and invite the Holy Spirit into our lives. Prayer simply helps us become more like Jesus! Daily prayer can bless you, your family, and others you pray for in your life. Prayer also invites more peace into your life. Prayer helps you learn more about God's plan for you and His will for your life.

There once were two men who set out on a boat to visit different areas of the world together. They ran into turbulent waters and ended up stranded on an island in the middle of nowhere. Being very religious, the two men decided to test out the power of prayer. "I'll live on the west side of the island, and you live in the east," one said, "We'll see if our prayers will truly be granted." The other man agreed and, after a brief goodbye, they set off to survive on their sides of the island. The first man knelt and prayed for food and shelter. He began wandering and found a warm, dry cave, suitable for a home. He also was able to find some bananas, coconuts, and fruit trees nearby. The other man, however, found himself in the part of the island covered with thick vines, with no safe place to stay or food in sight. The first man woke up in the morning and, feeling quite thirsty, prayed for water to drink. As he wandered around, he found a cool spring of crystal-clear water. And the other man found no water and felt himself weaken with thirst. After many months of living comfortably on the island, the first man felt lonely and prayed for a companion. The next morning, he found a woman passed out on the beach. The other man, however, felt his heart ache with loneliness, but there was no one to keep him company for miles around. Finally, after many years, the first man got bored with his life on the island and decided to return home. So, he prayed for this. The next day, he spotted an abandoned ship on the beach. The man and his wife packed up their things and got ready to go on the ship. But then God said, "Hold on! Don't you think you should bring your friend with you too? He has suffered much over these years." The first man, who had completely forgotten about the other man, was exasperated. "Lord," he said, "Why should I do that? He and I made a deal to try out the power of prayer, and, as far as I'm concerned, You answered all of mine, and You didn't answer any of his. I lived well; he suffered. That means his prayers weren't answered. So, really, why bother helping someone so unworthy?"

God got angry with him and said, "Don't be so arrogant! Your fellow is just as worthy of getting out of this island as you are, for I answered both your prayers." The first man was shocked. "What? You answered his prayers, Lord?" "Yes, I did. For his only prayer, all these years, was that all of yours would be granted."

(Note: Concept derived from a story called "Faith on an Island.")

The point of the story is that others are praying and interceding on behalf of our lives all the time; don't take that for granted, and always covet and cherish the prayers others pray for you. Our blessings are not the fruits of our prayers alone, but those of others praying for us. Prayer is one of the deepest forms of love.

The Serenity Prayer is something I circle back to many times in my life: 1) Acceptance of things I can not change, 2) Courage to change the things I can, and 3) Wisdom and discernment to know the difference.

Make *2025* A Year of Prayer: 1) Thank God, 2) Ask for God's will, 3) Say what you need, 4) Ask for forgiveness, 5) Pray with a close friend, 6) Pray over the Word of God, and 7) Memorize scripture.

Tasting the Fruits of the Spirit

Love, Joy, Peace, Patience, Kindness, Goodness, Faithfulness, Gentleness, and Self-Control: Love satisfies our deepest needs and is characteristic of God's love. Joy is felt each day, whether our circumstances are happy or not. Peace is felt in the midst of chaos in our lives. Patience is needed when society prefers immediate gratification and efficiency. Kindness is shown in even the most difficult situations. Goodness is demonstrated even in trying situations. Faithfulness is found on a foundation that is firm, stable, and steadfast. Gentleness is present even when you come up against opposition and adversity. Self-control is present even when you are being tempted in certain situations. We practice the Fruits of the Spirit in our interactions in our everyday life. Physical fruit needs time to grow, and the Fruit of the Spirit will not ripen in our lives overnight. Seeds are planted, and it takes time for them to come to fruition. We must constantly work to rid our lives of the "weeds" in them. The Holy Spirit gives us the Power to reject our old sinful nature.

My husband, Nate, leads within our home by encouraging us to pay attention to the Fruits of the Spirit and our attitudes and behavior toward one another. We have chosen one of the Fruits of the Spirit to meditate on and apply to our lives each month. Through specifically working on one of these at a time, it creates the environment of hope and inspiration that we will be able to move toward closer unity as a family. During family devotions, we can revisit the Fruit of the Spirit of the month and see how it applies to the scripture verse we are studying as a family at that time. This helps us all keep that one particular "fruit" at the forefront of our minds.

Scripture to Look Up in the Bible

Love: John 3:16; **Joy:** Romans 15:13; **Peace:** Hebrews 12:14; **Patience:** Ephesians 4:2; **Kindness:** Joel 2:13; **Goodness:** Psalm 23:6; **Faithfulness:** 2 Thessalonians 3:3; **Gentleness:** Colossians 3:12; and **Self-Control:** Titus 1:8.

The Power of Daily Journaling:

Treat Yourself to a New Journal and Start Writing Today!

Why is journaling so important? It helps us boost our mood and enhances our sense of well-being. It reduces symptoms of depression and improves your working memory. It also helps, in general, clarify your thoughts. What is effective journaling? Effective journaling is writing down what helps you meet your goals or improve the quality of your life. An example of effective journaling was when my husband and I went to Italy to celebrate the ten-year anniversary of our marriage. I wrote down interesting places we visited and the variety of food we tasted that day. I also included what the weather was like and memorable moments from the day. I jotted down thoughts, feelings, and reflections about each day.

The Acronym **WRITE** (Center for Journal Therapy)

W: What you want to write about

R: Review or reflect on it

I: Investigate your thoughts and feelings through your writing

T: Time yourself to ensure that you write for the amount of time your goal is

E: Exit strategy and with introspection

W: What's going on in your life, your current thoughts, what are you striving toward, what are you trying to avoid, prayer requests, and answers to prayer.

R: Take a few moments to be still and review or reflect on your life, catch your breath, and focus (mindfulness or meditation). Start with "I" statements and keep writing in the present tense.

I: Investigate your thoughts and feelings, write about where your mind starts to wander (take thoughts captive as necessary), take a moment to re-focus, read over what you have written, and continue on.

T: Time yourself, write for a specific amount of time, write down your start and finish time, and set an alarm for the time goal you have set.

E: Think about how you are going to exit writing, read what you wrote, reflect on it, and sum up with two sentences ("I'm aware of..." or "I feel...").

Scientific Research on Journaling (HOLSTEE)

Journaling can reduce depression and anxiety. It can help boost immune function and cultivate an attitude of gratitude. It can help with recovery from trauma and improve memory function. Journaling has been shown to have significant mental and physical health benefits and to improve a person's overall quality of life.

Charles Dickens was one of eight children and forced to leave school to work ten-hour days in a warehouse at age twelve. When he was a young man, he decided to be an actor. He missed his audition because he had a cold and settled on writing instead. He went on to become one of the most treasured authors throughout history.

Lessons & Reflection

1. Are there times when I struggle to see God's presence in difficult situations?
2. What steps can I take to strengthen my faith during times of uncertainty?
3. How can I emulate Jesus in my life?
4. What is my identity in Christ?
5. How does knowing my identity in Christ affect me?

_____

_____

_____

_____

_____

_____

_____

_____

_____

_____

_____

_____

CHAPTER 3

WHEN HER CUP RUNNETH OVER
(PERSEVERANCE)

Introduction: My Identity in Jesus Christ

Hello beautiful! My name is Carmen Maendel, and I am a child of God. I rededicated my life to Jesus Christ on November 04, 2006, after coming to the Lord at the very young age of thirteen. God has worked in amazing ways in the areas of fitness and nutrition, as well as overall wellness and self-care, in both my personal and professional life. I have an immense passion for this topic and devoted eight years of my life to training more than fifty women in our Maendel Fitness gym. God has guided and directed every step of the way from my initial certification of CFT and later Master's level in Nutrition, Precision Nutrition, and DNA Testing and Analysis to the process of acquiring each piece of equipment for the gym. I have prayed over every little and big decision involved in running our gym and spa. I was blessed with both the opportunity to do some sports and fitness modeling and become a founding member of the Men's Health Fitness Council in March of 2017. My goal is to share with you as many golden nuggets of fitness and nutrition knowledge and information for you to use and apply to your everyday life for wellness and self-care.

My Story: From Dim to Radiant and Glowing

A woman glows when she is loved, cared for, appreciated, feels useful to others, is working in an area she is deeply passionate about, and has Jesus in her heart. All women are beautiful regardless of their size, body type, or bone structure. Confidence is feeling amazing with the body God blessed you with, and respecting your body as the temple of the Holy Spirit. Confidence is your identity in Jesus Christ and not a number on a scale. It's all about rockin' what you got! I did not always have high energy and radiate great levels of confidence, as I do today, when I walk into a room. When I was a Freshman at Cornell College, I was away from home for the first time, and had terrible eating and exercise habits. I lived off vending machines and pizza during late-night crunches for writing papers and completing projects due the following day. My father was battling cancer, and my best friend crossed the centerline, hitting another vehicle head-on. She miraculously survived; however, her little brother and his fianceé did not. This was a very difficult time for me in life, and all my relationships suffered. I started to spiral down in a very unhealthy way. I knew I did not want to live like this forever, and I did something about it.

I began to run at the gym and get involved with as many sports activities at the college as I could, with my sorority or with friends at that time. I started avoiding the vending machines and late-night pizza, and paid attention to the food I ate at the cafeteria. The weight began to come off, and I started to feel healthier again. After college, I began working out regularly at the 24 Hour Fitness Gym and paying closer attention to my diet and exercise in general. One of the strategies I used for myself and my clients was the 80/20 Philosophy. Eighty percent of the time, pay close attention to what you eat and exercise, and twenty percent of the time, take a break from working out and eat what you like, in moderation. Moderation is the key to being able to eat whatever you like, whenever you want. As long as you eat smaller portions, you can enjoy some of your favorite foods that may have heavier fats, carbs, and sugars in them.

Maendel Fitness: Founding the Company in 2016

I began to view diet and exercise as a lifestyle. If you do something 21 days in a row successfully, it can start to become a habit. If you continue with healthy habits, making small tweaks here and there, it can become your lifestyle. As I learned all this amazing health and fitness information, I was passionate to learn even more and share it with others. After heavy prayer, I decided to open Maendel Fitness in 2016 after I achieved my Certified Fitness Trainer licensure with ISSA. I started helping my clients with a broad scope of the following: 1) Core Work, 2) HIIT Training, 3) Strength Training, and 4) Spiritual and Mind/Body Connection. We looked at Limiting Factors that may be standing in the way of them achieving their goals. Together, we put a plan together to help them break through some of the fears and barriers they had that were keeping them from achieving their fitness and nutrition goals. I also encouraged my clients to choose a Bible verse that they related to and were passionate about and recite it three times in the morning and evening. Writing affirmations and reciting them daily was also part of the program I created for myself earlier on and used with clients as well. We used SMART Goals and set three twelve-week goals together in the areas of fitness and nutrition. Through client feedback over the years, I realized how important it was for them to recite out loud the goals they had for themselves each day, three times in the morning and evening.

With God's guidance, I experienced major breakthroughs with my clients in the areas of confidence boosting and realizing they were capable of way more than they thought they were. I had them write out

"I can" statements and affirmations on paper and recite those as well. It was incredible to witness them moving from tears and not being able to write down a single thing to smiles and writing down a list of twenty-plus things they were capable of doing in our gym in a six-month period of time. I believed in the philosophy of "teaching them how to fish" instead of "giving them fish." This means that my desire was to have my clients graduate from my program, be able to create their own workout programs, and know their way around any gym they entered. I pushed them to their limits; however, I do understand that everyone has a limited capacity they can reach. I was sensitive to this and always tried to set my clients up for success and not failure. I had a rule that I would never ask my client to do something that I would not be able and willing to do myself. This created an enormous amount of trust and respect between us and helped them reach incredible new levels of fitness.

God has blessed me with the experience of eight years working side by side with women, helping them lose anywhere between twenty and sixty-plus pounds. I watched these women blossom into incredible, confident women. It was all-encompassing and not just about losing weight. I taught these women proper form in lifting weights, how to create their own HIIT Cardio and Strength Training workouts. I also have helped these same women with spiritual mind and body work as part of the nutrition training I did with them. Teaching my clients information about health and nutrition, while challenging them to reach different goals and continuing to set them up for success, not failure, is a true balance in lifestyle. I encouraged them to look at their spheres of influence in their lives and identify the things they had control of and the things they did not, and how to recognize the difference between the two. I also taught my clients that they did not have a problem with motivation; however, it was discipline that they struggled with. If someone feels like doing something, they do it when they are motivated to do it. However, when someone does something regardless of whether or not they feel like doing it, they are disciplined in that area. We can learn to discipline ourselves to be able to achieve various accomplishments in life.

For the remainder of this chapter, I would love to provide you with some tangible tips, tricks, and resources that God has revealed to me that you can use to embrace your own wellness journey. I will be drawing from various parts of my online fitness and nutrition program, Rock Hard Body - Power - Strength - Fitness, that I created in 2023. The foundation I liked to start with a client is the Spiritual component. I encouraged my clients to seek out their favorite Bible scripture, meditate on specific scriptures: Luke 18:27, Matthew 7:7, 1 Corinthians 2:9, Mark 11:23, Ephesians 4:23, Psalm 51:10, Proverbs 3:5, are all part of that foundation. We also talked throughout the upcoming sessions about working out their muscle of prayer, the Fruits of the Spirit, and the power of daily journaling. When I first started training clients in 2016, I did not emphasize the spiritual mind and body connection; however, in the last several years of training clients, I have. I always encouraged them in that direction, and if I felt any resistance at all, we would move away from it. I was surprised by how many of my clients in the last few years were very open to learning about the spiritual mind and body connection, and it helped them achieve their incredible fitness and nutrition results.

I established a baseline with them by measuring (neck, chest, waist, hips, right arm, right leg), weighing them with my bioelectrical scale percentages (weight, body fat, muscle, bone), measuring their height, and recording their body mass index (BMI), and taking before and after shots from the front, side, and back. We then sat down together and created three fitness goals and three twelve-week nutrition goals. I asked them to please recite these three times in the morning and evening out loud. I also encouraged them to create positive affirmations and "I Can" statements, reciting them out loud as well. As we progressed through the sessions, I taught them proper form for lifting weights and how to use the various machines and exercise equipment in our gym. As we worked on core strength, I taught them that one of the best ways to alleviate back pain is to strengthen their core muscles. The back and core work together, so if you have a weak core, you probably also have a weak back. The reverse is true also, so if you have a strong core, you have a strong back. It is very important to incorporate Core Strength Training into your workouts.

I also taught them how to create a HIIT High Intensity Interval Training portion of their workout. One easy 20–30 min HIIT workout could be the following: 3 min warm up—2 min HIIT followed by 1 min recovery—3 min cool down. Another one could be: 3 min warm up—10 sec HIIT followed by 50 sec recovery—3 min cool down. You can get creative with the intervals of HIIT and recovery. When you work out with HIIT Cardio, your oxygen level is at a higher rate, and your body begins to repair itself. As your body cools down, your metabolism speeds up and you burn more fat. HIIT Training is a very efficient way to exercise, and weight lifting is one component of HIIT Training. Why do we lift weights? The scientific reason why we lift weights is the following: building more muscle tissue increases your demand for glucose. The muscles pull glucose from your bloodstream so that your blood sugar levels do not rise to abnormal levels within your body. Recovery between sets, during workouts, between workout days, and on the weekends is very important when it comes to lifting weights.

God revealed to me through prayer that the spiritual mind and body connection is very important. I worked with clients with the mindset portion for fifteen minutes prior to training them for an hour in our gym. I taught them how to ditch their diet mentality and embrace healthy lifestyle choices for fitness and nutrition. Here are Five Ways to Embrace Change: 1) seek out new perspectives and be teachable, 2) do something new and exciting stretching yourself out of your comfort zone, 3) shed your old self and get rid of old negative habits, 4) replace the bad habits with positive ones, and 5) learn to live on faith and believe that good things are coming your way. Before we succeed in life, we first must be able to embrace change. Without change, growth is not possible. Forming good habits and being disciplined leads to feeling motivated; a huge transformation can then take place in your life. Here are a few examples of Healthy Lifestyle Choices: 1) park farther away from your destination and walk, 2) take the stairs over the elevator, 3) get up and walk around for breaks regularly, 4) fitness program of HIIT Cardio, Strength Training, and Core Strength, 5) emphasize core strength because a strong core leads to a strong body, 6) get 6–8 hours of sleep daily, especially deep sleep, 7) Eliminate or decrease stress in your life, and 8) drink at least 68 ounces of water throughout your day. Also, please don't hold on to the assumption that you can't grow and learn from past failures. You absolutely can learn from your past mistakes in life and be stronger moving forward. Most importantly, learn to operate and call upon God's strength and not your own.

Every obstacle you face offers an opportunity to improve. Pushing through challenging moments in life will help you reach a higher level. It may take us a while to accomplish something in life, but eventually we will succeed if we keep on trying. We can choose how we respond to adversity in our lives. We may not be able to control what happens to us in life; however, we can choose how we respond to what happens to us. "You miss one hundred percent of the shots you don't take" (Burton W. Kanter); "You can't hit the ball (get a hit) if you don't swing (the bat)" (Wayne Gretzky). The definition of self-confidence is a feeling of trust in one's abilities, qualities, and judgment. What if a person has low self-esteem and lacks self-confidence? Self-confidence is a skill that can be learned, practiced, and perfected in life. Self-confidence is something that we can all learn to master, given lots of practice, perseverance, reliance, and full trust in God. Our identity is in Christ and not ourselves. We need to learn how to place the focus on Jesus and not on ourselves. When we do this, our self-confidence and peace in Christ will soar to new heights.

God has taught me about the need for having control in my life. Learning about the spheres of control can be helpful in breaking barriers and reaching for success in your fitness and nutrition goals. There are three categories of control: 1) things you can control, 2) what you can influence, and 3) everything else outside of your control and influence. Learn to recognize the difference between these **three spheres of influence** and have peace with the things that are completely out of your control. God is completely in control of everything in our lives at all times. If we learn to trust Him fully, we can give up that need for control in our lives and gain more peace. We also need to get rid of limiting factors in our lives. There are false beliefs that are keeping you from crushing your goals and breaking through barriers in life. What are they? Some examples of limiting factors are the following: 1) wishful thinking instead of doing the hard work, 2) setting goals with unrealistic time frames, 3) lack of planning or having systems in place to track your progress, 4) lack of commitment or discipline, and 5) lack of perseverance and sustainability. Five Steps to Overcome These Limiting Factors: 1) establish a solid foundation for your goals, 2) set urgent but realistic time frames for goals, 3) set yourself up for success with proper systems in place and tracking devices to monitor your progress, 4) establish your "why" when confidence lessons, you can remind yourself why you are strongly committed to your goals, and 5) set yourself up with success with a plan of consistent sustainability once you hit your goals, so you can maintain your progress for a lifetime.

I was obedient to God's calling when He asked me to close Maendel Fitness and run Nate's Property Maintenance LLC alongside my husband. I feel blessed and honored to have gotten the eight years I did to work with and encourage women! Please feel free to use any of the resources I included for you below to help you achieve your ultimate fitness, nutrition, and wellness goals for self-care.

Positive Biblical Affirmations:

- **I am the Apple of His eye (Deuteronomy 32:10)**
- **I am Fearfully and Wonderfully made (Psalm 139:14)**
- **I am Kept in His perfect peace (Isaiah 26:3)**
- **I am an Overcomer (1 John 5:5)**
- **I am Redeemed (Ephesians 1:7)**
- **I am Yoked to a gentle Master (Matthew 11:29)**
- **I am the Temple of God the Holy Spirit (1 Corinthians 6:19)**
- **I am Purchased for God by the blood of Jesus (Revelation 5:9)**
- **I am Inseparable from the love of God in Christ Jesus (Romans 8:39)**

- **I am Sealed with the Holy Spirit (Ephesians 1:13)**
- **I am Eternally secure (John 6:39)**
- **I am Chosen from before the foundation of the world (Ephesians 1:4)**
- **I am a New creation in Christ (2 Corinthians 5:17)**
- **I am a Daughter of the King (John 1:12)**

Maendel Fitness: Fitness & Nutrition Resources

Carmen Maendel YouTube Channel

https://www.youtube.com/@carmenmaendel6186

MFC Muscle Menu

https://drive.google.com/file/d/1iob0qnW2TLD8CE7cj9gLx9jP8hG1Jcfn/view?usp=sharing

MFC Guru Grocery List

https://drive.google.com/file/d/1FHt77_tiJostf7lEKNYzbeYTEqAG7i1L/view?usp=sharing

MFC Tasty & Savory Cookbook

https://drive.google.com/file/d/1RItKdZqlntip1Bh7AEzC67020xQmrJ_k/view?usp=sharing

MFC Confidence Boost System

https://drive.google.com/file/d/1wo7usMTuOzO1y3YHEglm-r7wnAydP7cv/view?usp=sharing

MFC I Can Statements Worksheet

https://drive.google.com/file/d/1oSLTWLCWLpdw6xQEWBIkd9D3IfBCSpG3/view?usp=shar

Lessons & Reflection

1. What Bible verse do I relate to the most in my life?

2. How can I improve the connection between my physical and spiritual life?

3. How am I placing my health and wellness as a priority in my life?

4. What are some positive affirmations I could recite to myself on a daily basis?

5. What tangible things can I do each day to help boost my confidence overall?

CHAPTER 4

CLOTHED IN GOD'S RADIANT BEAUTY
(TRANSFORMATION)

My Story: From Ashes to Beauty

I did not always have the body, self-confidence, and exuberance I do today! I have not always had the opportunities opened up to me as a sports and fitness model or owning my own fitness business! I have not always looked like this or received constant positive reinforcement and attention when I walk into a room! There was a time that I struggled horribly with my weight and identity, and I want to talk about that time with you.

Some people gain the "freshman fifteen" in their first year of college, and I more than doubled that in my first year away from home. I had literally gained fifty pounds by the end of my second year. I was under a great deal of stress as my father was battling cancer, and I lost someone I loved very much to a car accident around that same time. My grades suffered, and I switched majors several times. I struggled with my identity, and every relationship in my life was strained in general. I continued to spiral down and feel a loss of control in every area of my life! On November 4, 2006, things began to change in my life when I came to the Lord and surrendered my heart to Him. I got married and we had a son shortly after. My relationships continued to improve, and I was able to drop all the weight I had gained in college and keep it off to this day.

Today, I feel very blessed to have the deep and intimate relationships I have with my closest friends and family. I feel well-grounded and know that my identity lies in Christ alone. Why do I share all this with you? I realize that it is not just who I am now that has helped coach over fifty women that I have since I opened Maendel Fitness in 2016. It is also the person I used to be, and the fact that I can relate to how many of you feel when you have difficulty getting dressed in the morning or just looking at yourself in the mirror. I know what that feels like because it used to be the same for me. I hope that you can be encouraged by me sharing all of this with you, and I hope and pray that this helps you dig deep down and discover your own identity in Christ, breaking free from any barriers or obstacles keeping you from your deepest desires, dreams, and aspirations!

How I Got From There to Where I Am Today: My Personal Christian Testimony

I grew up in the upper midwest portion of Iowa in a very peaceful country setting in Waterloo, Iowa. I come from a very affluent background, and my father was an Orthopedic surgeon practicing medicine in several different hospitals in the surrounding area. Surgeons of ophthalmology run several generations deep in our family. I grew up with my older sister, Kathleen, and brother, Jim, who we adopted from Vietnam. There was quite a bit of friendly sibling rivalry between the three of us. Our parents had a full-size indoor pool with sliding glass doors built as an addition to our home. The doors slid open all around it, creating an outdoor atmosphere as well. My sister and I especially used it for swimming laps and preparation for our upcoming swim team events. Our family enjoyed evening entertainment from going out to the theatre for plays and operas to hosting large groups of people in our home. We went on multiple vacations to Europe and enjoyed fine dining quite frequently. My father worked very hard for long hours and sadly passed away from cancer when he was still fairly young. Part of his legacy lives on today through the Phelps Youth Pavilion Children's Museum in Waterloo, Iowa, celebrating all the families he touched through operating on them over all those years.

Our father and mother did instill a very good work ethic in all of us through various chores we did around the home, and working in our acre garden, helping process vegetables to sell at the Farmers Market and freeze for our family. I remember having to process huge piles of peas, spinach, green beans, and corn on the picnic table before we were allowed to leave the house. We helped run the cattle through the shoots for various shots and maintenance about four times a year. Our family owned Dale G. Family Shorthorns company, which we raised at the time fifty head of cattle, which expanded in the years to come, for beef to sell each year. We also had a variety of different horses we owned and worked with on our property. I loved to ride horses, and I showed my Tennessee Walker, Ed, at the 4-H Fair. In middle school and high school, I was in the Fellowship of Christian Athletes and enjoyed the fellowship and playing sports. I remember "getting saved" in 9th grade; however, I did not really understand what all that meant at that time in my life. I remember the only church influence I had growing up was attending the Episcopal church with our grandparents on an occasional and sporadic basis.

College was the next phase of my life and still void of God. I got caught up in sorority and fraternity parties, clubs, and various social activities that surround the college scene at Cornell College. My father continued to battle cancer, and someone I loved very dearly died in a car accident around that same time as well! This was a very difficult time for me in life. I continued to spiral downward, and every single relationship in my life, I struggled with at that time. I was living off vending machines and late-night pizza, while turning in large projects and papers the next day. This was no way to live, and I knew I was meant for more. I knew even at that time, before I even understood Christ to the level I do today, that God had a better, more fulfilling purpose for my life. I cut out the late-night vending machine visits and started working out regularly at the college, and the Freshmen fifteen, times three, started to come off. Cancer runs on my father's side of the family, and strokes and diabetes run on my mom's side. The moment my father became unresponsive to cancer was the same moment I made a vow to myself to get into the very best possible physical shape that I could and stay there for life! I have been successful in doing just that!

While I was attending UW-Madison a few years later, I was approached by a woman named Vision. She invited me to a Bible study that I started attending regularly. There was somewhat of a language barrier as well since she was Korean and spoke very little English. For a while, God was at the forefront of my mind, and I kept searching for answers about life through Him. A few more years later, I began my fourth undergraduate degree at Stevens Point and returned to the college party scene once again. I was married to my first husband, a non-believer, who struggled with an addiction that I was not aware of at the time I married him. I attended six years of counseling with him, and when it became clear I wanted him to be healthier than he wanted to be himself, I left him. I was starting new at that time; a new career, a new car, and a new place to live. I taught Special Education for four years, and my contract was not renewed because I was one of the youngest teachers to come aboard, while some of the older ones were able to get tenure. One of the mothers of the students that I taught was the Regional Director of Edward Jones, and she recruited me into the wonderful field of finance. I soon started my eight-year career as a stockbroker and financial advisor. I drove a JAG, dressed the part in a three- to four-piece suit with my hair in a bun every day. I had similar aspirations as my father to become very wealthy; however, God had another very different and unique plan for my life.

Nathanael (Nate), the love of my life and husband of almost eighteen years today, was very instrumental in helping to bring me to Christ. I started attending Woodmen Valley Chapel in Colorado Springs, CO, when they changed their singles group meeting time from evenings to Sunday mornings. I started going to group Bible studies and group activities, which Nathanael also attended. I remember taking two seminars: 1) Starting Over and 2) Becoming the Right Person at Woodmen Valley Chapel. I found out later that Nathanael had taken them as well, prior to us getting married. He also had been previously married once, prior to us getting married to one another. I began having coffee at Starbucks with Nathanael after church on Sundays. I got deeper involved with church activities like hiking, Christian comedy, picnics, and church dances. I also started regularly attending evening Bible studies with Nathanael. Meanwhile, he changed the auto setting in my JAG to Christian music and would wait at the doorway of the clubs I attended, without ever setting foot into them himself.

I remember a turning point in my life, which was a very clear black-and-white God moment. Nathanael had invited me to a Halloween church dance, and I had already made plans to go downtown with my friends from JP Morgan Chase that evening to the clubs. I broke my plans with my friends, and I met Nathanael at the church dance instead. He and I made a real deep connection that night, and he was very helpful in answering all the questions I had about God, the Bible, and walking with the Lord. I began coming with him as he prepared firewood for his clients. I would sit in the truck and do devotions for hours, devouring the Bible as he was working outside. Slowly, I made the transition to helping him more and more with the business. Soon, I was splitting wood with the machine, helping him put up retaining walls, and even helping shovel rock for some landscape projects for Greens & Things, a far cry from the cushy lifestyle I had grown up in.

Black-to-White Transition: My Life After Fully Rededicating My Life to the Lord

It was November 4, 2006, in the evening, when we were visiting a friend's home, Mariana, that I re-dedicated my life to the Lord. She held my hands as I asked Jesus into my heart and to be Lord of my life. Nathanael and my friendship grew stronger, and after about a year, we began courting one another. We both shared dreams of doing world ministry and possibly owning a business as a family together someday. We were baptized at the same time together, at Woodmen Valley Chapel, several months prior to getting married on July 21, 2007.

I feel very blessed that God led me to Nathanael and his entire family. I love his parents as I love my own and always call them mom and dad. His dad sadly passed away in December 2021, unexpectedly, so he is no longer with us today. His dad and mom have helped guide me biblically through some very difficult trials in my life. When I married Nathanael, I also gained many brothers and sisters in Christ. I am very close to my brothers- and sisters-in-law on the Maendel side of the family. Two years after we were married, we received the miracle of giving birth to our beautiful little boy, Joshua. We tried for more children; however, in the process, we lost one set of twins and another baby in mid-pregnancy. We trust in God's plan for our family's future, and we eagerly and expectantly allow Him to guide our steps along the way.

God has blessed us with a beautiful home with acreage in the middle of Baxter, MN, to run our family business on today. He has remained faithful and has blessed our family immensely in many ways throughout the years. I realize that the one thing that I kept searching for over all these years was right there in front of me. I had filled that void with so many unhealthy choices and bad experiences in my life for so long because none of them were ever lifetime sustainable. Jesus is the only precious thing that can fill that void on so many different levels in multiple people's lives. I truly hope that you are inspired by reading my life story and seeing how many adversities and challenges I have navigated through during my life. I can not do it alone. I call upon Jesus' strength and not my own, and continue to search for peace, harmony, and joy through Him alone.

This brings me to today and the plan God has laid out before us. I previously owned Maendel Fitness for eight years and poured into my clients passionately in the areas of Strength Training, HIIT Cardio, Core Training, Mind-Body-Spiritual Connections, and DNA Testing and Analysis. I so enjoyed walking alongside these women, building relationships and trust, while witnessing their incredible transformations on the inside and out! I enjoyed all the connections and professional relationships God blessed me with while running that company. I even had the opportunity to do some sports and fitness modeling within the fitness industry for several years. I later decided against continuing on that modeling path into the future because it was becoming more about me and Maendel Fitness and less about Jesus.

My husband had been offered a position outside of this area, so we needed to place our home on the market and move quickly at that time. I was forced to shut down all gym and online services for Maendel Fitness Gym & Spa after putting my blood, sweat, and tears into this company for many years. I did not know at the time that God was going to ask me to run our current company, Nate's Property Maintenance LLC, right alongside my husband. I would never be able to enjoy the blessing of owning and running this company with my husband if I had dug my heels in and held on tightly to Maendel Fitness. God knows better what we really need in our lives than we do at all times. I encourage you all to meditate on Proverbs 3:5-6:

"Trust in the LORD with all your heart and lean not on your own understanding; in all your ways submit to him, and he will make your paths straight."

Lessons & Reflection

1. What recent situations or encounters have caused me to feel God's presence?

2. How has God guided me through the recent decisions I have made?

3. Are there recurring themes or patterns in my life that might indicate God's hand at work?

4. In what ways am I experiencing personal growth that could be attributed to God's influence?

5. How can I be more open to recognizing God's work in my daily life?

_____

_____

_____

_____

_____

_____

_____

_____

_____

_____

CHAPTER 5

GOD EMERGES FROM THE SHADOWS
(ENLIGHTENMENT)

My Identity in Christ: I Am a Child of God

I am Carmen Maendel and I am a child of God. God has blessed me with an incredible husband and son to travel through life with. Heaven is our true home and we are just passing through. Everything belongs to God, always has and always will. I want to preface that any accomplishments or accolades that have happened to me came from God, not me. Everything I do, I do for the glory of God. "I can do all things in Christ who strengthens me" (Philippians 4:13).

A Worldly View of Entrepreneurship: God Emerges from the Shadows

How do you view entrepreneurship? I have a very clear black-and-white difference of how I approached being an entrepreneur before and after I rededicated my life to Christ on November 4, 2006. In the upcoming narrative, I will demonstrate how I am clearly the shadow, the reflection of God, as He has created me in His image. I am nothing without God, and He is the one who gets all the glory, not me. As I began to learn more about God, I learned more about myself and my true identity. Everything belongs to God in the first place: money, accomplishments, business, time, loved ones, and all my possessions. As I came to this realization, I began to hold loosely to the things of this world and started investing toward the Kingdom. I moved from an attitude of "I did it" to

"God did it," and apart from Him, I am nothing. He receives all the praises and glory, not me.

Humble Beginnings: Entrepreneur as a Child

I remember setting up the lemonade stand and making sure everything on the table was positioned just right. My mother was watching from afar as these burly John Deere workers came up to purchase lemonade from me at the ripe age of four. With confidence, I would pour each glass and beam at the amount of money I was making at that time. My father was an orthopedic surgeon, and money was a very common topic amongst our family members at the dinner table. I am so thankful that, along with money, came the topic of a strong work ethic, too. My strong work ethic today, I know, comes from God and how my parents raised me from day one.

Another childhood entrepreneur example was when I set up all my stuff from my room with individual prices on them, for a kitchen table sale when my relatives came to visit. I would once again carefully place each item and make it look as appealing as I possibly could. I believe Grandma and Grandpa sometimes bought things from me just to humor me. They were my target clients and always came through for me. My grandfather was the one who, later in life, planted the initial financial seed in me. I got very interested in stocks, bonds, and trading on the market after watching him use the computer to do so. This interest led to my passion in finance and later career and endeavor as a stockbroker and financial advisor for eight years of my life.

One final example of child entrepreneurship was when my siblings and I combined with two childhood friends of ours, Bridget and David, would go weekly to the farmers market to sell vegetables from our garden. We raised the vegetables, prepared them for the market, and proceeded to sell them every Saturday growing up. This was an opportunity for my siblings and me to learn a strong work ethic and earn a little profit at a very young age. The groundwork had been laid for me to spring into my career as a financial advisor and stockbroker and earn a ton of money doing so, or so I thought. God intervened, introduced me to my husband of almost eighteen years today, and took my life on a very different course than I had ever imagined.

Seeing Dollar Signs: Entrepreneurship as an Adult

I graduated from multiple colleges and universities, and I was ready to go out and earn my "millions" in the world. I taught for several years, and when the enrollment dropped, my teaching contract was not renewed for the following year in special education. One of the mothers of the students I taught was the Executive Director of Edward Jones and recognized a unique gift and skill set I had for mathematics and numbers. I went through a vigorous interview process, including several rounds with panel interviews, and finally was offered the position of Stockbroker and Financial Advisor with their firm. My first taste in the business world was to go door-knocking every day for the next six months. I remember meeting some very interesting people in the process. I also remember learning to develop tougher skin and getting creative along the way. I remember one person in particular whom I knocked on their door, and they were extremely rude to me. Instead of feeling down, I kind of made a game out of it: "Who is behind door #3?" One time, when the person at the front door was rude, I simply went to the side and knocked again, while asking if there was a more polite person living on this side of their home. Gutsy move, yes; however, I believe they were a little convicted and embarrassed by the way they had treated me by the sheepish look on their face when they came to the door the second time.

Lessons Learned: The Golden Rule

I have learned that you always treat a client in the way that you want to be treated yourself, hence the Golden Rule. Don't ever give up! Your solution may be closer than you think. Like the man searching for gold who stopped mining three feet from where another miner struck gold! Learn not from your own understanding, but from Proverbs 3:5-6. When things look completely hopeless on your end, there may be a blessing in disguise waiting for you. This happened to me in the case of the storm damage that happened to me three times during the course of owning my gym for an eight-year period. God blessed us with complete waterproofing of our gym, Medical 4 Infrared Therapy, and a seven-person, J-275 Jacuzzi outback. We would have never been able to enjoy that blessing today if I had given up and thrown in the towel at the first sign of water in our gym.

Be solution-oriented and focus on the solution and not on the problem. Be creative and learn to think outside of the box, and be ready to collaborate and bounce ideas off of others in a similar field. Create a mastermind group to meet with and work through obstacles, turning stumbling blocks into stepping stones. Two heads are better than one! Learn to be flexible and patient with everyone. Things will go wrong in a company, and attitude is ninety percent of the solution, and learn how to deal with conflict well. It will certainly happen, and more importantly, it is how you react to something that is truly important. Learn to juggle multiple things at a time and get very good at time management, which will help you maximize your profits in business. Be ready to make sacrifices in some areas that may turn out to be difficult decisions. Always follow up and become an incredible listener, having the utmost respect for all your clients. If they have an issue with something, make it right! A few dollars eaten here and there are much better than any negative feedback about you and your company. Always operate with the strictest honor and integrity with those around you. Always treat others how you would want to be treated yourself! Be ready to take action with various opportunities that come your way! It is okay not to be a perfectionist, and it is actually better to learn flexibility and teachability instead. You will have to adapt to multiple situations in business, and being flexible and teachable goes a long way! Always get in the room with people who are smarter and more successful than you are because you can always learn something from them and may even have an opportunity to collaborate with them in some way, shape, or form. You can draw strength from your weaknesses, and ultimately, you should be drawing strength through God and not from your own strength.

Lessons Learned: Through Ownership of Four Companies

I learned many lessons while I owned Carmen Maendel Photography. I learned that sometimes you need to just capture the moment instead of waiting for all the right things to come together in your environment before hitting the button. You may miss the window and lose the opportunity for the shot if you wait for everything to be perfect around you before taking it. I have learned to simply slow down in life and smell the roses, and appreciate the beauty God has created around me while having a camera in my hand. I learned probably the most about trusting God and others during my ownership of Maendel Fitness Gym and Spa. I learned to read people and empathize (not sympathize) with each of their stories and individual experiences in life. By empathizing with them, I could demonstrate that I care; however, I was not going to be drawn into their drama. I learned to make sure I never asked my clients to do something that I was not willing or able to do myself. I would lead by example and encourage them to follow suit. I built trust and rapport with them and encouraged them to be the best versions of themselves. I encouraged them to only compete with themselves and not compare themselves to others. I also learned a great deal since 2009 while running Nate's Property Maintenance, renamed to Nate's Property Maintenance LLC. I learned about mutual respect with my husband, and that our company does not run smoothly if either one of us is pulled out of that equation. It takes both of us to complement one another in very different disciplines to be a power couple in business together. I have learned patience and flexibility when it comes to operating our company together. There are so many variables that can go right and wrong, and conflict resolution is much more important to understand than knowing exactly how to solve everything at once. It is important to work through some of these conflicts in business, and you feel a sense of accomplishment together when you do.

Entrepreneurship is like riding a roller coaster. You will have mountain tops to celebrate your victories together, and you will also have the valleys or trenches. The most growth will occur in the valleys and trenches, and if you persevere forward, it is all worth it in the end. My husband and I keep God in the center of all we do. We stop and pray before moving forward when we feel we have come to a cross in the road. We try to be logical and pray over things thoroughly instead of making impulsive decisions or actions. We have collaborated with various companies: ad specialists, realtors, builders, and other professionals as we continue to scale our company. I hope you can be inspired through my sharing some valuable tidbits about what I have learned personally as an entrepreneur for several years now. There are lessons and insights that we can learn from one another, so we do not repeat mistakes made in the past! The journey is so much more important than the destination. Entrepreneurship is not an overnight affair. It is not ordering Amazon Prime and having it delivered to your door in two days. It takes time, a business plan, a business strategy, and a whole lot of other components working simultaneously. It is two steps forward and one step back sometimes. It can be like the stock market and show volatility, lots of ups and downs over the course of time. It can provide freedom and monetary benefits that provide more choices for you and your family. It can be very satisfying and exciting to experience this with your spouse. It is completely worth it! Most importantly, I have learned that everything belongs to God and to keep Jesus at the center of your business at all times.

Seeing God Instead of Dollar Signs: The Entrepreneurial Flip

I view things very differently in business today. I realize that God is always in control in every situation in my life. This allows me to have peace in both my personal and business life. I do not need to worry about the daily happenings in our company. God has always been faithful, and He always will continue to be faithful in our lives. He expects us to be good stewards of what He blesses us with; that is our part. We need to let go after we do our part, get out of the way, and let Him do the rest! Since it all belongs to God anyway, each morning as I pray, I acknowledge that we don't have ownership in our company and we trust Him to guide and lead us in the correct direction. During my morning routine of working out in our gym, I incorporate praying for direction and guidance for myself in both my personal and business life. I also pray over my husband, son, family members, friends, and church family as well! If something comes up and I miss my normal routine of thirty minutes in prayer in our gym, I feel off that day. I have learned to trust in Jesus and allow Him to lead me as I run our company from home each day. Nate does the same as he is running our company from out in the field each day. We both will continue to have mutual respect for each other's contribution to our company, and value and cherish what we both bring to the table. Nate's Property Maintenance LLC would not be the same if either one of us were missing from the equation, and more importantly, if God were missing from the equation. I hope you can be inspired through my story of entrepreneurship, and I wish you all the very best in all your future endeavors!

> *"How God leads us and where He leads us will always be a bit of a mystery. But what doesn't have to be mysterious is this: We will see God's glory either on this side of eternity or on the other side."*
> — Lysa Terkeurst

Lessons & Reflection

1. What are my core values and my long-term life goals?
2. What makes me feel most fulfilled in life?
3. Who are the most important people in my life?
4. What are my biggest passions in life, and where do I see myself in 5 or 10 years?
5. What am I most proud of for achieving in life, and most excited about for my future?

_____

_____

_____

_____

_____

_____

_____

_____

_____

_____

_____

_____

_____

CHAPTER 6

WE DESPERATELY NEED JESUS
(FRUITS OF THE SPIRIT)

Nice Girl or Mean Girl?

Hello friend, I am Carmen Maendel, and I am a child of God. I am not perfect; only Jesus can be perfect! I make mistakes, mess up, make wrong judgment calls, jump to conclusions, have miscommunications, disagreements, and generally am what you call "flaw-some." I am full of flaws and awesome at the same time. I am perfectly imperfect! I am created in God's image, and I am exactly how He designed me to be. I also love to uplift, encourage, bond at a deep level with, walk alongside both women and men, and experience life with them as God intended us to do! I am incapable of surface-level friendships in my life because of how God has designed me to be. I have very few deep-level friendships in my life, with a plethora of acquaintances. My husband, Nate Maendel, is my closest and deepest soul-friendship connection and understands me like no one else on this earth. I am both a nice girl and a mean girl at the same time! There is an explanation for this in my upcoming chapter I am about to share with you!

The Middle School Debacle

I don't think middle school is easy for anyone. I remember this time very clearly in my mind, and it has helped shape me into the Godly woman that I am today. This is what I remember about middle school. I remember issues with female friendships and boys and the confusion of it all, simultaneously. I remember how everyone, including myself, was striving so hard to fit in that, at any expense, we would put others down in order to feel good about ourselves. I remember one thing very clearly at that time in my life. My horse, Ed, was my number one best friend, and he was loyal one hundred percent of the time. I remember coming home from school in tears nearly once or twice a week, and jumping on my horse, bareback, to run to the end of our property line. There were numerous stories told to my big, beautiful black Tennessee Walker at that time in my life. This period of time helped me grow thicker skin and become more resilient to many other life experiences I have had since then. I developed coping strategies for myself and a unique approach to lifting up and encouraging both women and men. At this point, I was both a nice girl and a mean girl for pure survival mode in middle school; however, I was leaning toward nice! By starting to take the focus off myself and placing it on others, I was able to feel empowered in various scenarios.

Discovery of the Fruits of the Spirit

College life and entrance into corporate America presented their own set of unique and precarious challenges. I experienced power struggles with both men and women, and a deep appreciation for differing views and interpretations of life at the same time. I was beginning to get a taste of and practice the Fruits of the Spirit before I even knew they existed. Love, Joy, Peace, Patience, Kindness, Goodness, Faithfulness, Gentleness, and Self-Control. God has provided many situations that I have had the ability to learn and practice the Fruits of the Spirit in my life. One experience I had was when I was still working as a Financial Advisor and Stockbroker, and that stuck out in my mind. I was kind of a mean girl and quite full of myself at this point in my life. My husband today refers to that time in my life when I was a "highfalutin" stockbroker. I admit it, I was a brat. I cared very little about other people and mostly about the profits I was making at the bank I was working at then. I drove my JAG, wore a three-piece suit, and had my hair up in a bun; I played the part well. I was a "top banker" financial advisor and stockbroker and made more money than any of the other bankers at that branch at that time. My co-workers were fed up with me and conspired a devious plan to get me out of the bank. This was the plan: they would wait until no one else in the bank had a license high enough to help a client with a stocks and bonds investment, but me. I was one of the few licensed bankers who worked there with a Series 7 Stock Broker license. Most of the other bankers I worked with just had their Series 6. Then, they would have me help Nate Maendel (who at that time in my life was simply a friend of mine and nothing else) with his investments over the lunch hour. They then brought me into the main office to speak to the corporate representative over the phone, more like interrogating me. I asked to have my attorney present, and they denied my request. They falsely accused me of helping a "family member" with an account at the bank, which would be an extreme conflict of interest; however, Nate Maendel, at that time in my life, was not a family member to me. They were successful in falsifying information and falsely accusing me of a Code of Conduct violation on my perfect, spotless U4. After consulting with my attorney, I put in my "resignation in lieu of termination" request shortly thereafter, and God removed me from my successful eight-year career in this field. Little did I know at the time that God was using Nate, my husband today, as a conduit to draw me away from a life and future filled with extreme materialism and idolatry. Directly following my leaving the bank, my life would take on a very different trajectory, embracing deep spiritual meaning and peace. In retrospect, several years later, after rededicating my life to the Lord on November 4,

2006, I approached one of my former co-workers from the bank, apologized for my despicable behavior back then, and asked for their forgiveness. It was a moment of mutual forgiveness for both of us, and peace was restored between us. We both won!

I also was given the opportunity to practice a full array of the Fruits of the Spirit when I owned my own gym and spa, Maendel Fitness. I loved how God would present various situations that gave me the opportunity to have patience and kindness towards my clients. I was able to form deep connections with over fifty women at the time that I owned and operated our gym. Every day was a lesson not only for my clients but for me as well, in love, gentleness, and self-control. I learned more about life in general during that period of time than at any other time in my life. I was deeply connected to God and my clients, and prayed for guidance and direction to help my fitness and nutrition clients break through all types of barriers. I remember working with specific clients for a year or so and developing such a deep bond, level of trust, and respect with each other that was insurmountable. I attributed all the success of my clients directly to my obedience to following the plan that God guided me to take. I spent those eight years deepening my relationship with God and my clients simultaneously. It is bittersweet as I look back upon those days of fellowship, incredible growth, and success with my Maendel Fitness and Nutrition clients. I knew exactly when to push and when to draw back a little, ensuring the highest sense of achievement in their programs. I knew this because I listened to God and followed the plan He laid out for me to train my clients. I always encouraged my clients to never compare themselves to anyone except themselves. I always said, "Aim at being a better version of yourself today than you were yesterday!" God guided me with the perfect mix of the Fruits of the

Spirit to help me mirror and match, encourage, push, and facilitate my clients to a higher level of fitness than they had ever had before. I am able to use this epiphany to learn, lead, and work with our clients today with Nate's Property Maintenance LLC.

This brings me to today, working with Nate's Property Maintenance LLC. I definitely achieve and have more of an abundance of peace in my life as a nice girl rather than a mean girl. There is so much truth to the saying, "You can catch more bees with honey than with vinegar." Nice girls really do finish first. My husband and I have multiple opportunities each day to exercise the Fruits of the Spirit with our clientele. I believe God has a sense of humor and will give us multiple scenarios with the same "fruit" to see if we finally get it. Nate and I have both been humbled by multiple situations in our business and personal lives. I am always quick to give grace, mercy, and forgiveness because I know that someday the tables may be turned, and I may be the one seeking the grace, mercy, and forgiveness from someone else. The more I try to put myself in someone's proverbial shoes, the more I have a deeper sense of empathy and love for that person. I have also realized that the thing that bothers me most about someone else is usually an underlying issue that I have not dealt with in myself. The Golden Rule always applies when working with my husband, our NPM Team, and our clients: "Do unto others as you would want them to do unto you."

I have included tips and tricks to being a nice girl and getting along and empowering others in both your personal and business life in the second half of this chapter, "We All Desperately Need Jesus," of this book. When we "win" in life, everyone "wins" as we continue to lift up, encourage, speak truth and positivity, motivate, walk alongside, and empower other women in our lives!

Nice Girl Attributes and Characteristics (28 Things I Have Learned in My Life)

1) Be Not Susceptible to Petty Jealousy

Jealousy can cause trust issues and insecurity in relationships, hindering both personal and mutual growth.

2) Be Dependable

A quality woman is true to her word and follows through after she promises to do something.

3) Be Honest

Honesty is a valued trait and plays a crucial role in every area of our lives.

4) Be Forgiving

Forgiveness is an attribute of strength, and holding a grudge only harms you and not the other person.

5) Be Kind and Compassionate

Treat everyone with respect, be empathetic to their pain, and help them in any way you can.

6) Be Positive

A quality woman has a positive outlook on life and does not perseverate on their problems.

7) Be A Good Listener

Be an excellent communicator and pay full attention to someone when they speak.

8) Be Funny and Entertaining

Be cheerful and lighthearted to help lighten up stressful situations in life.

9) Be Humble

Take constructive criticism to heart, accept your flaws, and work daily to improve yourself.

10) Be Supportive and Motivating

Support and encourage those around you to achieve their dreams.

11) Be in Charge of Your Life

Accept responsibility instead of making excuses and own up to your mistakes in life.

12) Be Respectful of Yourself and Others

Value and love yourself before you expect the world to do the same to you.

13) Be Responsible and Hardworking

Work diligently and responsibly to achieve your goals.

14) Be Independent

Do not rely on anyone outside of God for your happiness.

15) Be Loyal

Be faithful, stand up for what you believe in, and don't break trust with anyone.

16) Be Patient

Be patient and wait upon the Lord, and don't worry or complain during the process.

17) Be Fun and Energetic

Know when to let your hair down and have fun while you are achieving your goals.

18) Be Genuine

Stick to your authentic self and personality, and don't try to impress others around you.

19) Be Dignified

Respond to everything in a grown-up and dignified manner.

20) Be Aware and Steer Clear of Gossip

Do not speak badly about others behind their back, and stop someone from talking negatively about someone else.

21) Be Accepting of Your Imperfections

Do not look down on others, and encourage them to be a better version of themselves.

22) Be Open to Expressing Yourself

Have courage to express yourself, and open up to others you trust.

23) Be Ambitious

Setting and achieving goals, with God's guidance, gives purpose to your life.

24) Be Mindful of Your Health and Self-Care

Take care of yourself and your body while you are busy helping everyone else out as well.

25) Be Diligent About Choosing Your Circle of Friends

Choose your friends carefully because you become who you hang around, and reduce toxicity from your life.

26) Be Teachable and Knowledgeable

Always be open to learning new things and hearing different opinions from others.

27) Be Courageous

Have a strong will, speak up, and do not be afraid to say "no" to something that goes against your values.

28) Be Trustworthy

Be honest, genuine, keep your promises, and be approachable for those who trust and confide in you.

Lessons & Reflection

1. How would someone else, close to me, describe my personality?
2. How would I describe my personality and values?
3. What was a significant turning point in my life?
4. What is a lesson I learned from a past challenge?
5. What or who is the biggest influence on who I am today?

_____

_____

_____

_____

_____

_____

_____

_____

_____

_____

_____

_____

_____

_____

CHAPTER 7

WITH THE HELMET OF SALVATION
(SELF-CONFIDENCE)

Introduction: I Am a Child of God

Hello friend, I am Carmen Maendel, and I am a child of God, a wife, and a mother. I came to the Lord at the early age of thirteen; however, I rededicated my life to Christ as an adult on November 4, 2006. This does not mean that I am perfect or have not had adversity in my life. Quite the opposite, I would say. Some of the negative incidents in my life happen when I am seeking the Lord wholeheartedly. In this book, *Courageous Woman: Casting Cares Upon Jesus*, this chapter, "With the Helmet of Salvation," I will share some life-altering moments with you after I was saved and wear my "Helmet of Salvation" on a daily basis. My narrative begins, prior to my rededication to Christ, with a traumatic event that God uses for His Glory to help me train over fifty women in our Maendel Fitness Gym & Spa several years later.

Grocery Store Incident: Creepy Men Stalking Me

It was a normal day for me, working as a Stockbroker and Financial Advisor at that time. I have always aimed at maintaining a specific structure in my life, and to this day develop daily routines and systems that help my day run more smoothly and productively. I left the office and headed to a commercial gym to work out. I had just invested in a lifetime membership with this gym and felt pretty good about putting all this in place to increase my likelihood of staying invested in my workouts. I finished my workout and began to walk to my car to go home that evening. I knew the grocery store was right behind the gym, so I stopped off to grab a few items on the way home. This is where the nightmare began. I was standing in the checkout lane, and a guy from the gym, who taught self-defense, was standing right behind me. He told me, "There are three men who have been following you in this store." I had an immediate choice to make in whether I was going to trust and believe him, or think that he may have some part in all this, too. He asked me, "Would you like me to walk you out to your car tonight?" I decided that a friendly face from the gym was more inviting than having three men tailing me out to my car.

As we walked out to my car, I noticed that the three men that he told me about had parked immediately across from my JAG and were slinking away in their seats, watching me. They wore blue jeans, baseball caps, and orange-colored down vests that night. I asked the guy who was walking me to my car to please stay with me, as my heart was beginning to race, and I had determined that these three men were definitely up to no good. He proceeded to help me put my groceries in the car and then sat down in the driver's seat as I got into the passenger seat. He started my car and pulled it around to the back of the store, and we called the police immediately. The police came, but those three men took off long before they even got there. Tags were spotted on their vehicle, and it turned out they were from some country town outside of Colorado Springs, CO. I remember being very afraid that night to go back alone to my apartment. I called up a friend of mine, and they came over immediately and stayed that night to make sure I was alright. It is amazing how violated I felt even when none of them touched me. It was the fear of what might have happened that encouraged me to take steps toward empowerment and defend myself in any given scenario. To this day, I am very vigilant in paying attention to anyone who seems like they are following me. The next day, I enrolled in a Russian Self-Defense class and learned some techniques that would help defend myself if anything like this were to happen again in my life. I didn't even know God to the extent that I do today, and He protected me that evening by placing that man behind me in the grocery store. This incident, coupled with the next event I share with you, is what helped fuel my desire and passion to build a gym in our home today.

The Other Half of the Equation: My Father's Battle with Cancer

The other half of the equation for building the gym in our home came from the experience of my dad going into a state of unresponsiveness with his cancer. He fought long and hard for his life for about fifteen years. Coming from a medical background, he was able to try all the innovative medical technology and unique treatments for cancer. What had started out as prostate cancer had moved into other areas of his body and metastasized to the bone. By this time, his doctor described his cancer as throwing seeds into a field, and they just grew and grew at that point without ceasing. He became unresponsive at the later stages of his cancer, which finally spread to his brain. He was an orthopedic surgeon and understood what was happening to him. He was very aggravated and seemed to understand medically what was happening to him, and yet he had no control over it. I vowed to myself, that night, that I was going to get myself into the best possible physical condition I could and maintain that throughout my lifetime. Cancer runs on my father's side of the family, and we have lost several family members to it. Diabetes and strokes run on my mother's side, too, so I figured I would get myself into top physical condition and stay there for life in case something ever happened to me. I am glad I did because I did encounter several more medical challenges in my life that I will talk about in this chapter and book as well.

Passion for Health and Fitness: HHFM Ministry and Maendel Fitness

I knew after my terrifying experience of being stalked that I would no longer ever want to belong to a commercial gym again. I have always had a passion for health and fitness, so the only logical solution seemed to be creating our own gym space in the basement of the home my husband and I purchased here in Minnesota. I started to purchase a few items for the gym and began working out regularly. I felt guilty that this big, beautiful gym space was only being used by me. I started to invite friends over one by one to come work out with me in our gym. This led to me officially starting HHFM Heritage Health and Fitness Ministry in our church at that time. We had five or six ladies come work out regularly, once or twice a week, together. It was an amazing fellowship and an incredible way God used for me to begin to connect with women and exercise in a deep and meaningful way. I remember having about five Airdyne Schwinn bikes and doing HIIT High Intensity Interval Training workouts and cycling classes with them. We even had a room connected, dedicated to childcare, for the women working out in our gym. I led this ministry for about four years prior to deciding to attain my certificate as a Certified Fitness Trainer in 2016. This was the same year that I founded Maendel Fitness and started working with fitness clients in our basement gym. I realized that it was important to combine both fitness and nutrition, so I also got my Master's level in Nutrition and DNA Testing a few years later. God helped me work with my clients and achieve major breakthroughs in their lives that went way beyond just losing weight on a scale.

Vibrant You: Elevating Your Self-Confidence with Affirmations and Self-Love

Some of the things I worked on with my clients helped them elevate their confidence with affirmations and self-love. I asked them to pick a verse in the Bible that they believed in and could stand strong with. We also worked on affirmations and "I Can" statements to help reinforce their confidence in the things they could do and deflected those things that they could not do. I taught them that every obstacle that they face offers an opportunity to improve. I encouraged them to look at adversity in their lives as opportunities with solutions instead of problems and stumbling blocks in their lives. Pushing through challenging moments in your life will help you reach a higher level. It may take us a while to accomplish something in life, but eventually we will succeed if we keep on trying. According to Burton Kanter, "You miss one hundred percent of the shots you don't take." You need to just keep swinging and not give up! "You can't hit the ball (get a hit) if you don't swing (the bat)," Wayne Gretzky. The definition of self-confidence is the feeling of trust in one's abilities, qualities, and judgment. What if you are a person who suffers from low self-esteem and lacks self-confidence? I have good news for you! Self-confidence is a skill. Self-confidence is something that we can all learn to master, given lots of practice and perseverance. Whatever that thing is that you feel weak at, spend more time on that than any other activity, and you will improve over time. Self-confidence is an attitude about your skills and abilities. It means you accept and trust yourself and God, and have a sense of control in your life. You know your strengths and weaknesses very well, and still have a positive view of yourself.

Keys to Self-Confidence

1. Recognize what you excel at
2. Build positive relationships
3. Be kind to yourself
4. Learn to be assertive
5. Learn to say "no"
6. Give yourself challenges
7. Surround yourself with positive people
8. Take care of your body
9. Practice positive self-talk
10. Face your fears
11. Be in competition with only yourself
12. Stop comparing yourself to others

Four Areas This Can Have a Positive Effect on Our Lives

1) Better performance at work or in the home:

You don't waste time worrying that you are not good enough; instead, you can devote all your energy to your efforts, which lead to better performance.

2) Healthy relationships:

It impacts how you feel about yourself, and it helps you better understand and love others. It also gives us the strength to walk away if we are not being treated well.

3) Openness to try new things:

When you believe in yourself, you will be open to trying new things.

4) Resilience:

Believing in yourself can enhance your resilience and ability to recover from any challenges or adversities you face in life.

Keys to Affirmation

Words that lift you and others up: positive words about self or others; feel-good words; emotional support words; encouraging words.

Self-Affirmations

1. I am worth all the love I receive.
2. I am a beautiful creation.
3. I can handle all the challenges that I encounter.
4. I can do great things.
5. I am going to be successful.
6. I will not let failures get the best of me.

More Positive Affirmations

I have a purpose and was created with divine intention.

I can and I will... end of story.

My mind, body, and soul are super healthy.

I overcome my fears by meeting them head-on.

I feed my spirit and feed my body at the same time.

I am in charge of my own life through the decisions I make.

I will not compare myself to others in person or on the internet.

I am choosing and doing instead of sitting and wishing.

I am enough.

I am loved and cherished.

I have the power, within myself, to create change.

I believe good things are coming into my life.

I am strong and can get through anything in life with God by my side.

I will accomplish all that I set out to conquer in life with God's strength and not my own.

I request my desires through prayer, and I am ready to receive them all.

I am going to make you so proud of me.

I am powerful and strong.

I am truly unstoppable.

I go after what I want, and I get it when it aligns with God's will for my life.

I forgive those who have harmed me in the past.

I am the architect of my own life, and God directs my steps.

Story: The Architect

I want to share a story with you that I also shared with my fitness and nutrition clients about their lives. So, there once was a man who was an incredible architect. Whenever there was an extremely challenging project, this architect was brought on to lead the project. For many years, he built the most amazing buildings and structures around. He was even called in from out of state for specific, intricate building projects as well. After doing this for over thirty years, he came to his boss and told him, "I think this will be my final project as I am looking to move into other areas of my life right now." His boss was very sorry to see him go; however, he had deep respect for him and understood why he wanted to leave the firm. His boss asked him, "I have one final project I would love for you to do for me, and then you are free to go." So, the man set out to complete his final project. Materials were scarce and very expensive, so he found himself cutting corners on this project like he never would have even dreamed about doing on his former projects through the years. He raced through this one without doing his best work. He mostly just cared about finishing it and being done. Finally, the project was completed, and he walked into his boss's office to tell him that he was done. His boss gave him a hug and thanked him for all the long, hard years he had put into this firm. He then said, "Here, I want you to have the keys to this home you just created; it is my gift to you." Suddenly, the architect felt a sick feeling in his stomach. Had he known his boss was going to give him this home, he would have put much more effort into this project. He would have used much nicer material and not cut corners on the quality of craftsmanship involved in building this home. Did you know that the average person puts more thought into planning a vacation than into the details of living their lives? Don't make the same mistake that this architect did. Make sure you plan carefully the details of your life. "We may make our plans, but the Lord determines our steps" (Proverbs 16:9).

Building Maendel Fitness: Adversity and Obstacles Along the Way

I can recall four major setbacks that happened as I was building the gym and training clients over the eight-year period that I did. The first setback was the storm damage that happened to our gym. I remember laying down towels on the basement floor, and they would be soaked an hour later. I remember standing in the gym with tears rolling down my face and my friend hugging me and reassuring me that everything would be alright. We did two full remodels in the gym, only to have the same problem happen again. This happened on two occasions in spring, and the final time it happened, we decided to invest in very expensive drain tile around our gym and basement in general to save my company, Maendel Fitness. We also invested in a triple-safe sump pump system. I remember continuing to train my annual clients upstairs in our living-entertainment room in our make-shift gym for about three months while they were repairing the gym. If I had thrown in the towel, I would never have seen the plans God had for us to expand our gym into the spa/sauna area and a seven-person Jacuzzi out back.

The next setback was that I had injured my back earlier in life and re-injured it while I was swinging on a hammock that Nate and I had brought back from Mexico. I was swinging very high on his hammock, and our son, Josh, was watching me. All of a sudden, the hammock snapped and I went flying to the ground. I had numerous issues with my back after that, and almost even looked at back surgery as a solution to my problem. We realized that the bed we were sleeping on did not have the excellent back support that I needed; it had a broken board underneath. We replaced the board, and slowly, I began to heal again. I remember my sister-in-law sold me their tread climber that their family had bought some time ago and never used. I used this machine to try to increase the strength in my core, along with specific core exercises, without putting any pressure on my back. The core and the back work together, so if you have a weak core, you automatically also have a weak back. To this day, I make sure I have a very strong core and back so that I am not as susceptible to back injuries in my future.

The next setback was right before we did our grand reopening of Maendel Fitness after it had been remodeled for the second time. I was in the gym with my friend and her daughter. I had done an intensive hour-long kickboxing workout before they even got there. We started working out on the gym equipment, doing a cardio HIIT circuit training workout. I remember I was working out on the rowing machine, and all of a sudden, I told my friend, "I have had enough." She was surprised because usually she called me the Energizer Bunny when it came to working out. Her daughter then spilled some water on the gym floor. Because of our past history with water in the gym, I freaked out and jumped up to find a towel to clean it up. I ran into the laundry room right next door and luckily found a towel. If I had run upstairs, there is a chance that I might have fallen down those stairs unconscious. What happened next, I asked my friend to tell me, as I was unconscious myself.

Apparently, after grabbing the towel, I came into the gym and was standing holding the corner of the wooden beam. I fell directly backwards, hitting my head on the Airdyne bike peg. If the peg had not been there, I would have fallen directly on the back of my head onto the concrete floor. God protected me from this happening. I was knocked out for a few moments, and my friend told me that my body went into convulsions. I came to and realized that blood was streaming down the back of my neck. My friend took me immediately into the ER with a towel wrapped tightly around my head. As we were driving there, I was worried that I had suffered memory loss, so I kept asking her questions that she would know the answer to. She finally said to me, "Carmen, if you are asking me these questions, then you clearly don't have memory loss." We got to the hospital, and my husband greeted me with a rubber plant and a beautiful card. The doctor put seven staples in the back of my head that day. My doctor suspected that my blood pressure dropped because I had not eaten enough that day, and was drinking tea with Stevia in it. I have a very low athletic blood pressure anyway, and Stevia may have lowered it to an unsafe level and caused me to pass out.

I was afraid to work out in the gym that I had created, listening to God guide me along the way. This was a bit ironic. I was a fitness and nutrition trainer who was afraid to work out alone in our gym. I continued to train fitness and nutrition clients in our gym and kept this incident very quiet at that time, so none of my clients knew about it. I slowly built up my confidence to work out alone in our gym again. I began by making sure I always had my phone with me in the gym so that if something ever did happen, I could get help. I started with very short workouts just to prove to myself that I can do this. I eventually made them into longer workouts and started training regularly in our gym again. I knew if I did not "get back up on the horse" again after being bucked off, that I never would. Still to this day, I get up at 5:50 a.m. for my workout so that I can complete it before my son and husband leave our home, and I always take my phone with me to the gym.

So, this brings me to the final incident while owning Maendel Fitness. The winter of 2021 was a very difficult time for all of us. We had lost my husband's brother earlier that year, and Nate's dad, who I was super close to, passed away on December 8, 2021. I was able to have one final conversation with Dad on the phone the morning before he passed away; however, I had a serious case of COVID-19 pneumonia, so I was not able to go with our family to the hospital to say goodbye. For the entire month of December into January, I was laid up on the sofa in our family room. I remember sitting on the edge of our bed, gasping for air with the bedroom window open. I was the sickest I have ever been in my entire life and probably should have gone into the hospital. I stuck it out at home, and our son stayed home from school and took care of me while Nate was working outside our home. Our son, Josh, would make me soup, different dishes, and my green smoothies to try to help me get my strength back. I literally could not stand up for a while to make a meal. Our church family was very kind and brought in all different meals for all of us during that time. I remember setting the timer on the hour so that I would go out to our landing in the garage and practice breathing for one minute. I would take a deep inhale and then slowly allow the air to come out. I would repeat this process for about one minute. My brother-in-law, Dana, knew quite a bit about health and wellness, so he brought me a concoction of pills and liquids that truly did help me get better. I will always remember that period when our gym was shut down completely by our Minnesota governor during COVID, and God had some big plans for the gym shortly after that time.

Story: Three Feet from Gold (Napoleon Hill)

I have one final story for you that I hope serves as encouragement to you. There was once a man who was very dedicated to finding gold out west. He had moved his family out there, and they panned for gold every single day for twenty years. He found small hints of gold but never found anything extremely valuable. One day, he told his wife, "That's it, I'm done!" He had spent all that time looking for gold and never found it, and he was throwing in the towel. He packed up his family and left the next day. That same day, a young, energetic gold miner showed up to take over his spot for mining gold. He moved over just a little bit and struck gold that day. The first miner was three feet from striking gold, and he gave up. If he had had a little more staying power and discipline, he might have been the one who struck gold that day. Never, never, never give up! Your destination or goal may be closer than you think, and you will never know because you gave up! "Keep on swingin'... don't ever stop!"

Maendel Fitness: Fitness & Nutrition Resources

Carmen Maendel YouTube Channel

https://www.youtube.com/@carmenmaendel6186

MFC Muscle Menu

https://drive.google.com/file/d/1iob0qnW2TLD8CE7cj9gLx9jP8hG1Jcfn/view?usp=sharing

MFC Guru Grocery List

https://drive.google.com/file/d/1FHt77_tiJostf7lEKNYzbeYTEqAG7i1L/view?usp=sharing

MFC Tasty & Savory Cookbook

https://drive.google.com/file/d/1RItKdZqlntip1Bh7AEzC67020xQmrJ_k/view?usp=sharing

MFC Confidence Boost System

https://drive.google.com/file/d/1wo7usMTuOzO1y3YHEglm-r7wnAydP7cv/view?usp=sharing

MFC I Can Statements Worksheet

https://drive.google.com/file/d/1oSLTWLCWLpdw6xQEWBIkd9D3IfBCSpG3/view?usp=shar

Lessons & Reflection

1. What is a moment in my life that was negative that God turned around for good?
2. What are the areas in my life where I feel stuck or unfulfilled?
3. What negative self-talk do I often have about myself or my abilities?
4. What positive affirmations could help me cultivate a new belief?
5. How can I start to act in alignment with this new belief?

_____

_____

_____

_____

_____

_____

_____

_____

_____

_____

_____

_____

CHAPTER 8

WITH THE BREASTPLATE OF RIGHTEOUSNESS
(BLUEPRINT)

Introduction: Child of God

Hello friend, I am Carmen Maendel, and I am a child of God, a wife, and a mother. I came to the Lord at the early age of thirteen; however, I rededicated my life to Christ as an adult on November 4, 2006. This does not mean that I am perfect or have not had adversity in my life. Quite the opposite, I would say. Some of the negative incidents in my life happen when I am seeking the Lord wholeheartedly. In this book, *Courageous Woman: Casting Cares Upon Jesus*, I share my chapter, "With the Breastplate of Righteousness," with stories to help illustrate some of the adversity and challenges I have overcome in life. I hope and pray that these can be an encouragement to you in your own life journey as well.

My Story: The Downward Spiral

My story begins as I moved away to college, and for the first time, I was free to make whatever decisions I wanted with my life. Some of them were good and honorable, and others were not. My father was battling cancer, and someone I loved very dearly died in a car accident during my second year of college. This was a very difficult time for me, and I started some incredibly bad habits when it came to my health. I would stay up long hours writing papers and completing projects, and the vending machine became my "best friend" at that time. I was not getting the exercise I needed and was falling into a deeper pit when it came to believing in myself and having self-confidence in who I was and what I was doing with my life. I changed my major from pre-med to art and business, and still was very unclear about what my future would look like. I continued on this downward spiral, and it affected every relationship in my life. I struggled with having a good relationship with my parents, my siblings, my friends, and my boyfriend in college at that time. I felt numb and like I was just floating through life and not appreciating or valuing anything in my life at that time. It was not until I had graduated from that first college that I began to put my life back together again. I thought it was me doing this; however, in retrospect, I realize that God had never taken His hand off my life, even before I knew who He was. He had protected me in so many different situations that I could have really gotten myself into trouble, and the Holy Spirit continues to guide and direct me today. On November 4, 2006, I rededicated my life to Jesus, and things began to get better in my life. I was able to drop the fifty pounds I had gained in college and have been able to maintain that same level of fitness up until today. I created a plan for myself that I also used to help encourage and walk alongside my clients, to lose weight and feel better about themselves.

My Plan: Fitness and Nutrition Combined with Self-Love and Empowerment

I started working out daily in the gym or running outside, and paid attention to what I was eating. I cut out snacks, pizza, fast food, and junk food from my life entirely. I began healthy habits, which became my lifestyle to this day. Did you know that if you do something 21 days in a row and then 90 days after that, it can become a habit (a routine of behavior that is repeated regularly and tends to occur subconsciously) and part of your lifestyle—**21/90 Rule** by Dr. Maxwell Maltz. After spending the summer in England, France, and Spain, I realized that the Europeans were on to something when I came to eat and exercise daily. While I was in Spain, we had a small breakfast of fruit, meat, cheese, and bread. The lunch was the main meal of the day and consisted of a heavy dose of protein and carbohydrates. Dinner was very late, about 9 p.m., preceded by tapas or hors d'oeuvres a little earlier in the evening. Dinner usually was a small sandwich with meat and cheese. I loved their idea of eating a larger meal in the middle of the day instead of the evening, so it had time to burn it off during the day. Today, I incorporated a large salad for my meal in the middle of the day. I add meat and almonds to a mixed salad with carbohydrates, fats, and protein already. I usually have a smaller breakfast and dinner, incorporating all the food groups, in order to maintain a healthy lifestyle.

The **80/20 Rule, "The Pareto Principle"** by Vilfredo Pareto, is something I have incorporated into my lifestyle as well. Eighty percent of the time, I pay attention to exercise and eating healthy, and twenty percent of the time, I take a break from all of it and enjoy a cheat meal from time to time. Just remember this: "Always follow a cheat meal with a healthy one," and you can get back on track fairly easily. One part of my twenty percent every day is two pieces of dark chocolate. This helps me from building up a craving for chocolate over a period of time. I have always believed in routines and systems as they help keep me organized and moving in the right direction during the day. I usually get up at 5:50 a.m. every day, except on the weekends. The weekends are part of my twenty percent. I have a cereal bar with my vitamins and a green smoothie before my workout. I go down the stairs to our gym, where I have my workout clothes already laid out for me. I change and begin either a Strength Training, HIIT Cardio, or Core workout for about thirty to forty-five minutes each day. I spend this time in the gym praying for my friends, family, and church family. After coming upstairs from my workout, the first thing I do is have devotions for about thirty minutes. This time with God is necessary, and if I miss it in the morning, I definitely feel it throughout the day. I then move into a routine of getting dressed and ready for my day. I have specific systems and procedures in place daily for opening and closing our books, checking and zeroing out email, balancing our business account and filing receipts, and checking for leads. This is a quick snapshot of my daily routine.

As I reached my own goals and helped my Maendel Fitness clients, I developed three goals in the areas of fitness and nutrition. I used **SMART Goals** (Specific, Measurable, Attainable, Realistic, Timed) by George T. Doran to set various goals for myself and clients. For instance, a **Fitness Goal:** I will do a HIIT workout on the treadmill for thirty minutes every Monday, Wednesday, and Friday for the next six months with 100% accuracy. An example of a **Nutrition Goal:** I will incorporate one large salad into my diet every day for the next six months with 100% accuracy. I recited these goals three times out loud, and encouraged my clients to do the same, in the morning and evening on a daily basis.

I will share a secret with you that I found out about myself. Changing your lifestyle for the better has more to do with discipline than motivation. If you are motivated to do something, then you will stick to it when you feel like doing it. However, if you have the discipline to do something, you will do it regardless of whether you feel like doing it or not. "I would argue that it is not motivation alone that helps you achieve your goals; discipline plays a very large role as well!"—Carmen Maendel, ISSA CFT, CNS, PN1. While intrinsic/extrinsic motivation is built into your DNA, discipline is something that you can learn to do through continuous practice. Forming good habits and being disciplined lead to feeling motivated; a huge transformation can then take place in your life. A mindset shift can and will take place. You will begin to change your negative thoughts into positive ones. An example of this may be the following: "I don't like to be challenged" changed to "I want to challenge myself." Our greatest weakness lies in giving up. The most certain way to succeed in life is to always try just one more time!

Sometimes, you need to break through **limiting factors** (anything that is keeping you from achieving your goals) to believe that you are capable of doing something. You are responsible for yourself. The only one to limit your growth is you. You are the only one who can influence your success. Your life changes when you break through your limiting beliefs. You are in control of a large percentage of your life by the choices you make. You can not control what happens to you; however, you can control how you react to it. Ten percent is what happens to you in life, and 90 percent is how you react to it or your **attitude** about it. Are you going to keep allowing that person **(you)** to hold you back? We can choose how we respond to adversity in our lives. We can either let it break us down, or we can stand up to it and learn from it. We can respond in a way that limits us, or in a more productive way that potentially opens other windows of opportunity to us. I have learned that life is full of ups and downs and wins and losses.

Adversity is a large part of this experience and can be seen as a stumbling block or a stepping stone, depending on how you react to it. Adversity does not have to be a negative thing. You have the freedom to choose how you respond. You will encounter wins, losses, victories, and setbacks during life and your fitness journey; embrace them as they are all part of your fitness experience.

Examples of Possible Limiting Factors

Wishful thinking vs. doing the hard work

Setting goals with an unrealistic time frame

Lack of planning or having systems in place to track your progress

Lack of commitment or discipline

Lack of perseverance or sustainability

My bone structure is too big

I am not an athletic person

This is way too hard for me

I can't lose weight

I have zero desire to go to the gym

Some people have won the genetic lottery, and I have not

It is impossible for me to stay in shape after reaching a certain age

The only way I can lose weight is by stopping eating altogether

It's a genetic thing for me

It is just my fate to be like this

If I am ever able to lose weight, I will just get it right back

It's too expensive for me to stay in shape

It takes too much of my time

Diet programs are too complicated for me to follow

Carbohydrates make me fat

I must have an insulin-resistant problem

It's not that important to me to be in top physical shape

I don't like healthy foods

I can't afford healthy foods

I have a large body frame

Now that we've got that out of our system, **LET'S GET TO WORK!**

5 Steps to Overcome Limiting Factors

1. Establish a solid foundation for your goals instead of "wishful thinking"
2. Set an urgent but realistic time frame to accomplish these goals
3. Set yourself up for success with proper systems in place and tracking devices to monitor your progress
4. Establish your "why" when your confidence lessens; you can remind yourself why you are strongly committed to your goals
5. Set yourself up for success with a plan of consistent sustainability once you hit your goals, so you can maintain your progress for a lifetime

I have also adopted an idea from Dean Graziosi that I want to leave you with about the "**7 Layers of 'Why'**" concept. The way this works is you ask yourself seven layers deep why you are doing something in your life. An example of this is the following: 1) **Why am I passionate about health and fitness?** Because I like to have more energy for the things I love in life. 2) **Why do I like to have more energy for the things I love in life?** Because then I will have more quality time with our family. 3) **Why do I want to have more quality time with our family?** Because this brings more unity to our family. 4) **Why is more unity in** our family important?** Because we have more peace and quality of life together. 5) **Why is it important to have more peace and quality of life together?** Because honoring your father and mother is biblical and the right thing to do. 6) **Why is honoring your father and mother important?** Because when our son honors his dad and me, he also honors God. 7) **Why is it important to honor God?** Because we are made in His image for the specific purpose of honoring, worshiping, and praising Him. This is my seven levels of "why."

"Wishing you the very best in all your future endeavors, Beautiful!"

Lessons & Reflection

1. What is my dream job, and what are my career aspirations?
2. What is my ideal relationship dynamic?
3. What are my priorities for my spiritual, physical, mental, and emotional health?
4. How do I contribute to my community?
5. What legacy do I want to leave behind?

_____

_____

_____

_____

_____

_____

_____

_____

_____

_____

_____

_____

_____

Personal Reflection

God has taught me many lessons. I have learned to love and trust God with everything that occurs in my life: the good, the bad, and the ugly. I have learned to not trust my own heart, and that it can be desperately wicked and deceive me without even knowing it. I have learned that God is omnipotent and omnipresent, and knows things are going to happen before I do. Thus, trying to hide anything from God is completely senseless and futile on my part. If God closes a door, there is a reason for it, and He has something much better in mind for me. I have learned to have reverence and respect for my husband, and never take for granted everything that he does for me and our son. I have learned to hold loosely everything and everyone that God has blessed me with in life. It all belongs to Him in the first place. I have learned from Jesus' example that the best leaders are servant leaders who lead by example and serve others. The way to succeed in life is through helping and serving others, and placing their needs before my own. I have learned about mercy, grace, and forgiveness, and how important it is to quickly forgive and not hold onto grudges in my life. I have learned that the only prisoner is myself, thrown into bitterness and grief, when I do not forgive others. I have learned that the tables can turn very quickly, and the golden rule applies: "Do unto others as you would want them to do unto you." I have watched God remove people that I love dearly, heal some in miraculous ways, and allow very difficult and painful scenarios to occur in their lives and my own. I have learned to surrender it all over to Jesus, and trust fully that He knows better than I do what I truly need in my life. This means that I have a lot of unanswered prayers, emotional heartache, and even physically painful moments or trials occurring throughout the span of my lifetime. I embrace them all, and I am thankful for them all, including the hard times. This is my opportunity to experience a minute amount of pain that Jesus must have experienced Himself when He died on the cross for our sins. He took the punishment all upon Himself, dying on the cross and defeating death, so that we could have eternal life and the gift of the Holy Spirit guiding and directing us along the way. I have learned that no matter what I have accomplished in life, I need to point that all back to Jesus. I am nothing without Him, and He deserves all the accolades, praise, and adoration, not me. I know that God has my back and places a hedge of protection around me every day of my life.

Romans 8:28

"God works all things for the good of those who love Him, according to His purpose."

Interview Process

The next part of this book is going to be devoted to sharing the heartfelt true stories of women who were kind enough to openly and transparently share with me some incredible stories in their own lives. They have pointed to various ways that Jesus Christ has shown up and made huge, monumental differences in their lives. As I began my interview process, I gave the ladies four different options of how they would like to have their name appear in this book: 1) full name, 2) first name, 3) last name, and 4) other aliases. Some of the women were more willing to share their hard, raw truths, given they had some privacy built into the process. This is completely understandable, and I have the utmost respect for these women and the choices they made in the varying degrees of revealing themselves, directly connected to their stories.

I created several questions that would get to the heart of how Jesus Christ has worked in their lives, and I am very excited to share with all of you these incredible stories of these courageous women of God. Here are the questions that were posed using an in-person recorded interview setting or through email, depending on the geographical location of each woman.

1. How has Jesus most impacted your life?
2. What is the most painful incident that you have gone through in your life?
3. How did Jesus show up and encourage you through that experience in your life?
4. Describe your story and how Jesus turned something potentially bad into good.

5. What is your relationship to Jesus today?

6. How do you nurture your relationship with Jesus on a daily basis?

7. What talents and gifts have you received from the Lord?

8. How are you using those talents and gifts to help others?

My process included recording each individual interview (in person or over the phone), and some women emailed responses to my questions. This way, I did not miss any pertinent information that these women shared with me. Then, I listened to their stories multiple times, making sure that I was representing them and their stories with incredible accuracy. These women have trusted and confided in me with very personal information about their lives. I do not hold this process lightly as it is honoring all of these women and, ultimately, Jesus Christ, our Lord.

The stories will be divided across the following categories:

Chapter 9: Faith & Grace & Mercy
Chapter 10: Faith & Healing & Restoration
Chapter 11: Faith & Hope & Prayer
Chapter 12: Faith & Loss & Devastation

CHAPTER 9

FAITH & GRACE & MERCY

Hannah E.

Hannah has a steadfast faith in Jesus Christ and has been raised with the church since she was a young child. Jesus is her Rock, and she enjoys studying God's Word deeply: to learn, to share, and to teach. Hannah opted to email her responses to my "Jesus Questions" to me, and she gave me permission to share her story in this book, using the responses she emailed back to me.

Hannah remembers that day like it was yesterday. To those around her, it was a day like any other as her siblings and new friends gathered to worship, eat, play games, and laugh together at this quaint family camp nestled in the mountains of Pennsylvania. It was a day that changed her life forever. She grew up in a quiet, loving Christian home where her family went to church and did their best to live by Romans 12:18, "If possible, so far as it depends on you, live peaceably with all." She was by no means perfect, but getting into trouble devastated her, and she did her best to avoid it. Hannah believed in God and tried to please others so that she would find acceptance from her peers. Friendships were hard for her to make and keep as they moved a few times before she even got into the fourth grade. Hanna stated, "I was a quiet goody two-shoes." She was the target of bullies in first and second grade, and when her family finally settled in a permanent home in another state, it did not get any easier for her at school. She hated always being picked last in gym class. She commented, "It hurt when my peers started shouting 'Satan' in my face in the hallways." She went on to explain that she was not invited to any parties or social events. To make matters worse, Hanna found herself as the target of yet another bully. Since she was trying to live at peace with everyone, it took a couple of years before her teachers would believe her and make sure she did not share any classes with this bully in the future. Her few other friendships were a struggle to maintain at that time as well. Hanna shared, "Someone would be a friend to me one day and then turn their back on me permanently the next. I could not understand why this was happening to me?" She felt that she was a nice, giving, and loving person, and she felt very hopeless in this situation. Her mom was great and did what she could to help her process through the bullying, but it wasn't enough. Hannah longed for the love and acceptance of her peers.

So, there she was, sitting in the pew of the chapel, in the mountains of Pennsylvania, as a seventh grader with her grandma, siblings, and her new friends, feeling pretty good about herself. Hannah shared, "I had friends, I was having fun, and I confidently believed in God." The missionary who was preaching that day spoke about a dark, cluttered, and dirty basement with a window so filthy that no light could enter, illuminating the mess that needed to be cleaned up. The missionary spoke about how, when we give our lives to Jesus and make Him Lord over our lives, He not only cleans the window; He helps clean that basement, too! He spoke this truth, "Jesus is the light that enables us to see the sin we have cluttering the hidden places of our lives." When he was done preaching, he asked, "Who needs a Savior and Lord to let the light in and help clean that basement?" The conviction of the Holy Spirit hit Hannah HARD! She was a good kid who believed in Jesus, and everyone knew that. She shared, "It would be so embarrassing to walk down that aisle and admit that I needed more than just belief." James 2:19, "You believe that God is one; you do well. Even the demons believe-and-shudder!"

After a few moments that felt like an eternity, Hannah knew that she needed to follow the call of the Holy Spirit and reject the call of the Enemy of her soul. She commented, "I went forward, knelt, and asked Jesus to clean my basement window and be Lord of my life. I knew immediately that He had done just that." She had truly been forgiven, cleansed, and made new. 1 Peter 1:3-4 states, "Blessed be the God the Father of our Lord Jesus Christ! According to his great mercy, he has caused us to be born again to a living hope through the resurrection of Jesus Christ from the dead, to an inheritance that is imperishable, undefiled, and unfading, kept in heaven for you." Hannah shared, "I was born again, and born into a living hope!"

Her situation at school did not change; however, the way she responded to it began to change. She continued to face rejection and bullying to the point where her parents had to involve the police in this matter. She had started to receive threatening phone calls in high school from these bullies. Hannah shared, "Everything that her mom had been teaching her through the years of bullying and loneliness started to make sense." Her mom taught her how to have and show grace to others. Her mother explained to Hannah, "We have no idea what kind of home life or experiences this particular girl had, and we can not see the whole picture; we only saw what she was experiencing with you. God, however, knows the 'why' behind what she was doing, and He has the power to change hearts and minds." Hannah shared next, "He changed mine, after all. Instead of living in fear and anger, I needed to pray for her and all the others who had rejected and hurt me." As she did this, knowing the grace and mercy God had shown her in her own life, she began to pray for her enemies in accordance with Matthew 5:44, "Love your enemies and pray for those who persecute you."

Her mom taught her to give others the benefit of the doubt and let go of minor offenses. She doesn't know what happened to the girl who bullied her, but by the time they all graduated, she seemed content to leave Hannah alone. Hannah shared, "I have not seen her since, but have occasionally prayed for her as she comes to mind. I truly hope to meet her in heaven one day and hear how God transformed her life."

Three years into college and Hannah married the love of her life. Her husband had a love for theology and knew his Bible well. They shared a desire to do ministry in the church. For the next several years, they worked together in the church with various ministries, including children's ministry. Her husband did some preaching as well when their church was between pastors.

The time finally came when her husband was offered a pastorate in a tiny church a couple of hours away from where they lived at that time. There were both some very wonderful and some very difficult times during the three years they were there. Hannah stated, "As anyone who has been involved in ministry for any period of time knows, things rarely go easily or according to our hopes and dreams." She went on to explain that we have an enemy bent on stopping the Gospel message from going forth, and he will use anyone he can to accomplish that plan. 1 Peter 5:8, "Be sober minded; be watchful. Your enemy the devil prowls around like a roaring lion, seeking someone to devour."

At the end of three years, they faced a denominational leader who was critical of how they did their ministry. He wanted someone else in the church who was more willing to do what he thought was best to fill the position. Deciding that they could not live up to the expectations that were upon them, they stepped down and moved back to their old home and church they had been part of for many years. Hannah commented, "Unfortunately, but not surprisingly, Satan was working overtime to destroy us." Our former pastor chose to insult my husband instead of helping him, refusing his support, and effectively driving us from our old home church." Hannah was deeply hurt and angry at this time. She had dear friends in the women's Bible study for three years while they were in the ministry, who were lifting them up in prayer and encouraging her to remain in the Word, in prayer, and in faithfulness to God. Ephesians 3:16-20, "That according to the riches of his glory he may grant you to be strengthened with power through his Spirit in your inner being, so that Christ may dwell in your hearts through faith, that you, being rooted and grounded in love, may have strength to comprehend with all the saints what is the breadth and length and depth, and to know the love of Christ that surpasses knowledge, that you may be filled with all the fullness of God. Now to him who is able to do far more abundantly than all that we ask or think, according to the power at work within us."

As she remembered the lessons her mom had taught her all those years ago, and God heard the prayers of her faithful friends, she knew the power within her, through the Holy Spirit, allowed Christ to dwell in her heart through her faith. Hannah shared, "I was able to stay rooted and grounded in love. I struggled with anger toward the men who hurt us so deeply, but I was able to return again and again to prayer for my own heart, my husband, and for them." She did not know all the details of what was going on in their lives, but she did know that God is forever faithful not only to deal with the junk in her basement, but also with the junk in the basement of those men as well. She realized that harboring anger and resentment just cluttered her basement more, but did nothing to clean their basements. Hannah commented, "My heart was filled with love and grace and a willingness to forgive, even if trust was lost. I know well that this is not the normal response of a heart that has been betrayed, but it is the healing response of a heart rooted and grounded in the love of God and filled with the power of the Holy Spirit."

In many ways, this was a launching point for many other times of suffering in their lives; however, the lessons the Lord has taught them along the way were invaluable. Hannah knows that as humans with a selfish bent and free will, she knows that they will have trouble in this life. We will be persecuted and sinned against. James 1:13-15, "Let no one say when he is tempted, 'I am being tempted by God.' For God cannot be tempted with evil, and He himself tempts no one. But each person is tempted when he is lured and enticed by his own desire. Then desire when it has conceived gives birth to sin, and sin when it is full-grown brings forth death."

2 Timothy 3:12-15, "Indeed all who desire to live a Godly life in Christ Jesus will be persecuted, while evil people and imposters will go on from bad to worse, deceiving and being deceived. But as for you, continue in what you have learned and have firmly believed, knowing from who you learned it and how from childhood you have been acquainted with the sacred writings, which are able to make you wise for salvation through faith in Christ Jesus."

Hannah goes on to explain, "As we face persecution from both the world and from within the church, as believers, they let their guards down and give in to the temptations of selfishness and pride. We can rest assured that while God did not cause the sin, because He did not tempt anyone to sin, He does use the pain and the hurt to make us more like Jesus, as we place that pain in his hands."

James 1:2-4, "Count it all joy, my brothers, when you meet trials of various kinds, for you know that the testing of your faith produces steadfastness. And let steadfastness have its full effect, that you may be perfect and complete, lacking in nothing."

2 Corinthians 4:16-18, "So we do not lose heart. Though our outer self is easing away, our inner self is being renewed day by day. For this light momentary affliction is preparing for us an eternal weight of glory beyond all comparison as we look not to the things that are seen, but to the things that are unseen. For the things that are seen are transient, but the things that are unseen are eternal."

Hanna shares Ephesians 1:4, "It is the testing of the faith that allows us to become holy and blameless before him to be perfect and complete as James 1 says, and to be prepared for that eternal weight of glory beyond all comparison as 2 Corinthians says. It is so easy in our sufferings to become angry and bitter." Ephesians 4:26-27, "Be angry and do not sin, do not let the sun go down on your anger, and give no opportunity to the Devil."

Hannah goes on to explain that the devil is always looking for those he can devour. The last place she wants to find herself is in a place of bitterness, allowing the enemy to consume her joy and hope. When she is faithful in daily studying the Bible and praying for others, she finds the ability to live out Philippians 4:4-8 much more easily: "Rejoice in the Lord always; again I will say, rejoice. Let your reasonableness be known to everyone. The Lord is at hand; do not be anxious about anything but in everything by prayer and supplication with thanksgiving let your requests be made known to God. And the peace of God which surpasses all understanding, will guard your hearts and your minds in Christ Jesus. Finally, brothers, whatever is true, whatever is honorable, whatever is just, whatever is pure, whatever is lovely, whatever is commendable, if there is anything worthy of praise, think about these things."

She reflects on her years of joy and suffering. She has seen Jesus grow in her and has gained a deeper understanding of Scripture, desiring to share His truths with anyone else who is struggling and in need of hope. Hannah comments, "God has given me the immense blessing in the two Bible studies I am in right now to study God's Word deeply, to learn, to share, and to teach. Knowing the loneliness I have felt, God has blessed me with the ability to encourage and uplift friends in their faith through what He has taught me; to help them connect to others who can bless and encourage them as well."

Hannah shares, "Is it always easy to trust God in the midst of suffering? No. Is it always easy to have a strong and unshakable faith when the spin cycle gets hit in my life again? No. However, I have learned that in the darkest of times, God provides, and He will not let us suffer pointlessly. Through all the pain, we can be comforted." Romans 8:28, "That for those that love God all things work together for good, for those who are called according to His purpose."

Hannah draws to a close, commenting, "He has provided friends who point my eyes back to Him, a church body that comes alongside to pray with me, a pastor who faithfully teaches the Word of God, a husband who helps me see when I am being petty, and most of all, His Word.

Isaiah 30:15, 'For thus says the Lord God, the Holy one of Israel: In returning and rest you shall be saved, In quietness and confidence shall be your strength.'"

Hannah feels that the very best thing she can do as she prays through suffering is to make sure that she is not harboring any sin, and then to rest in the Lord, to be quiet, and to trust the Lord to work. Hannah closes with this comment, "After all, this life is not about my rights, my happiness, or drawing attention to myself, but rather about experiencing the joy and peace that happens as I seek to bring glory to God and make His name known."

Matthew 5:39

"But I tell you, do not resist an evil person. If anyone slaps you on the right cheek, turn to them the other cheek also."

Mary

Mary is a strong and courageous woman of God. She has endured a very difficult childhood and demonstrated extreme courage, mercy, and grace as she presented her story to me. Mary opted for an in-person interview and gave me permission to record our session together. I had forwarded my "Jesus Questions" to her beforehand, so she was well prepared to share her responses with me. I hope I can bring justice to Mary's testimony story and the deep connection she has with Jesus today.

While other children are playing outside and getting encouraging feedback daily from their parents, Mary was not. Her father was extremely physically and emotionally abusive to Mary and her siblings. Mary shared, "I was very fearful all the time. I knew the abuse was coming, and there was nothing I could do to stop it." She was dragged by her hair and beaten regularly. She was told by her father, "I hate you more and more each day." Her father reiterated how useless she was and how much he hated her all the time. Mary heard this so often that she began to believe these horrible things about herself, even when they were not true. The abuse became so severe for Mary and her siblings that she could not wait to get out of the house. Mary commented, "Eighteen became my magic number because I knew at that point I would be an adult and could make decisions for myself." When she turned eighteen, she did leave that home and all the brokenness behind her. She had to sneak away because her father would have never permitted her to leave. She packed a bag and whatever she could hold in her arms, and out she went. She met her husband the day she walked out of the house, and he took care of her immensely from that day forward. He treats her like she is the daughter of our Most High King, which she is indeed. Mary's relationship with her husband is incredible today, and they continue to take very good care of one another.

Fast forward a few years, and the most painful incident occurred in Mary and her husband's lives. Mary shared, "Our precious son committed suicide and this was probably the most painful incident we have ever endured in our lifetime; we were completely broken by this." God comforted her and her husband through all the painful details of this devastating occurrence in their lives. Mary had learned that God could be trusted even if her earthly father could not. Both of them leaned heavily on the Lord for comfort after losing their son to suicide. Jesus also has helped Mary heal from all the trauma and abuse from her past.

Mary shared her experience of how they ended up at the church they are now: "I remember seeing Pastor B preach at another location, and I was so impressed with him and the anointing God placed on him that we sought out the church he preached at; here we are today." Both Mary and her husband consider themselves tremendously blessed to have found a Bible-based church that excels in the preaching and teaching of the Word. Mary shared, "Jesus is my all in all!! I share Jesus with any opportunity I get. I get such satisfaction through helping people." Sometimes, this is received very well, and other times it is not, which is to be expected when we live in a broken world. Mary enjoys helping people with their pain they are going through in life in any way that she can. She has a heart of gold and a passion to love and encourage others. Mary comments, "I understand their pain and empathize with what they are going through using real-life experiences from my past." Jesus continues to heal Mary from all the trauma, physical, and mental abuse from her past. She dives into the Word daily and enjoys conversations centered around Jesus with her husband and other believers. She participates in a Women's Bible study that gives her the opportunity to have fellowship and deep conversations about Jesus with like-minded Christian women as well. Mary has chosen to follow Jesus for life!

Romans 1:18

"God knows about the trauma experienced by every single person. He knows the details of how the trauma came about, and He hates the wickedness that caused such pain. Take heart in knowing that God comforts us. He is close to the brokenhearted and comforts us when we suffer, holding us in His arms."

Shirley Braaten

Shirley Braaten is a courageous woman of God with an immense desire to help others. Our families have known each other for multiple decades and have remained very close friends. One of her sons was even my husband's best friend growing up. I am so excited that Shirley was eager to help me with my book project by sharing her real-life experiences with Jesus Christ. Shirley opted to email her responses to my "Jesus Questions" to me, and she gave me permission to share her story in this book, using the responses she emailed back to me.

Shirley shared, "Jesus is my all in all, without Him I wouldn't have been able to go through some of the difficult challenges of life that I have experienced in my seventy-plus years here on earth." She knows the eternal outcome has gotten her through, as she knows one day, because of what Jesus did for us, paying the ultimate cost, she will have eternal life. Shirley accepted His gift of salvation when she believed in her heart that Jesus was Lord and repented of her sins, so that she would have the precious gift of eternal life.

There have been several painful incidents that Shirley has gone through during her life. There is one in particular that had a strong impact when her sons were involved in a very life-threatening car accident. Shirley commented, "I knew that it was only by the grace of God that we received the favorable outcome that we did." Hearing that her son may not live, and if he did live, that he could have permanent brain damage, put her on her knees. The outreach from other Christians throughout the country, letting them know they were praying for their son and family, was an encouragement to them and illustrated what Jesus could do through His believers. Shirley shared, "I know that Jesus was present guiding us through this situation, because looking back, I have thought many times, *how did I get through this?*" Jesus guided her as she was shown the extent of her son's injuries, and then his need to be transferred down to the Children's Hospital in the city. They had to find someone to care for their other two sons and travel many miles to the Children's Hospital to wait for the outcome of their son. Shirley shared, "The waiting after our son had surgery to see what damage had been done to our son's brain was a hard one, BUT God helped us through this with His sustaining peace and comfort." They were again jolted into the reality of what a terrible outcome could have happened when they heard a Code Blue call to their son's room. What a relief to them both when they found out that their son was starting to come out of his coma; he had pulled out his breathing tube, and that was what had triggered the alarm to go off.

As their son started his road to recovery, while still not knowing for sure if there would be any lasting disabilities, Shirley shared, "We needed to lean totally on knowing that God was in control and He had us covered." As our son's recovery progressed, it became evident that our son had no lasting disabilities. Today, he is serving the Lord in his church, teaching young boys about the Lord and leading worship time. Shirley shared, "I have been able to share my experience to help others who are going through difficult times in their lives that God is good all the time, and having Jesus as your Lord and Savior, you can lean on His saving grace to get you through those difficult times." Shirley's relationship is steadfast in the Lord, knowing that in all things she needs to give it to the Lord, whether it is good or bad things happening at that moment. She shared Philippians 4:13, "I can do all things in Christ who strengthens me." Shirley reads God's Word and prays daily, usually praying multiple times throughout the day to nurture her precious relationship with Jesus. She stated, "If I don't start my day this way, I won't have a good day." Also, she makes sure to surround herself with Christian influences from both friends and family who uplift the power of God's love. This encourages her to know that they are praying for her and speaking His Word to her. They attend a good Bible believing church and are being fed God's Word through preaching and teaching on a regular basis. Shirley also leads a Ladies Sunday School class, which helps her dig deep into the Scriptures and discuss them with other ladies of Faith.

Shirley commented, "I pray I am a good listener to let those who are hurting feel comfortable coming to me, for getting help, using God's Word for direction in their life." This is an area that God has gifted Shirley tremendously. She shared, "I do love to help others and want to be God's servant in this area." She continues to use these God given talents and abilities to be there for others in their time of need. She does this by leading Ladies Sunday School class and having a time of fellowship with ladies in need, keeping an open-door policy for anyone who may need an ear to listen to them, and giving words of encouragement through God's Word.

Jeremiah 29:11

"For I know the plans I have for you, declares the Lord, plans to prosper you and not harm you, plans to give you hope and a future."

Traci Galles

Traci Galles is a courageous woman of God with a vibrant heart for the Lord. Her resilience and tenacity shine through in the midst of the adversity and challenges she has had in her life. Traci does not let her past dictate her future! She is a child of God through and through. Our families have known each other and remained close friends over the last decade or so. We have had the privilege of seeing her get married to Adam, and their family blossom and grow with the addition of their precious daughter, Nevaeh, being born. Traci opted to email her responses to my "Jesus Questions" to me, and she gave me permission to share her story in this book, using the responses she emailed back to me.

Traci grew up in Grand Rapids, Minnesota, with her two sisters and brother. She was surrounded by love in that home, and her father was a pastor of four separate churches in Minnesota. Her story begins with a heartbreaking incident when she was molested by a friend's nephew when she was eight years old. She shared, "He was a wrestler and told me if I told anyone, he would hurt me physically." This was a lot for an eight-year-old to take in; this has continued to haunt her to this day. Traci commented, "I still get nightmares from that experience."

Her family moved to Brainerd, Minnesota, when she was a senior in high school in 1994. When Traci turned twenty-one, she loved the Lord and cherished the mindset of being a virgin until she was married. This came to an abrupt halt when Traci was raped during that year. Traci went on to say, "I did not want anything to do with God at this point in my life." She drank heavily every weekend and lived a reckless and lackadaisical lifestyle. Traci lived with her mom, at that time, in a small apartment in 1998. Traci commented, "She ended up kicking me out because I was up until 4 a.m., and she had to work the next day." Traci contacted a friend of hers who lived in Richmond, Virginia, and that friend invited her to move there. Traci ended up moving there and living with that friend and her boyfriend for seven years.

Four natural disasters occurred while Traci was living in Richmond, Virginia. Traci shared, "After the fact, I realized that God had me experience those natural disasters because He wanted me to be home in Minnesota, where my family lived." She moved back home to Minnesota in September of 2008. She continued to adapt to Minnesota and worked a couple of different jobs there. Traci commented, "I was not very happy with random jobs." In May of 2010, Traci accepted a career offer at a very large hospital in Minnesota. She worked there for ten years in a very fulfilling position, and then she got laid off because of COVID.

A quick side story: This is a testament to Traci and her extreme perseverance and courage. On August 17, 2012, Traci Galles and Carmen Maendel were both recognized and interviewed by Renee Richardson with the Brainerd Dispatch newspaper. Renee wrote, "Driven by a passion to work for themselves, two area women create their own company." Genoa Denim & Leather Apparel was founded by Carmen and Traci. They formed their own online and trade show company designed to offer fashion to women at reasonable and reduced prices. They traveled around the state together, for various trade shows, selling their designer jeans and purses in 2012. They sold their company, for a profit, to Underground Apparel in Brainerd, MN, at the end of that year.

When Traci was laid off because of COVID, this affected her tremendously. Traci shared, "I was fine with it at first, but then a couple of weeks went by and I was devastated. It was one of the hardest and most difficult experiences that I've ever dealt with." The loss of Traci's job, after having that for ten years, sent her spiraling down into a deep depression. Traci shared, "Manic episodes of highs and lows accompanied by hallucinations..." She ended up in the hospital for seven days. This was an extremely difficult time for Traci. She shared, "It was very difficult to be away from my husband of ten years and daughter." She was really depressed because she had gained twenty pounds due to the medication she was taking. In retrospect, Traci realized she was hyper-focused on herself instead of others, "When you focus on others and their problems while having sympathy for them, that can help you in your own life."

In May of 2024, Traci experienced a severe headache with a pain level of ten, which was the highest level of pain. She was admitted to the hospital for three days until they were able to diagnose her with Lyme's disease and meningitis. She left the hospital on the fourth day, with doctor-prescribed pain medication, probiotics, and one antibiotic. That following week, her doctor in the ER called and recommended that she go to Fargo or Duluth hospital to treat a possible aneurysm. Traci and her husband decided to have the angiogram done at the St. Cloud hospital, and the results came back as "no findings." Traci shared, "We were really happy about that."

Today, Traci and her husband, Adam, lead a mental health group that they started in 2022. Traci spends a lot of time in the Word and shares Jesus with everyone she meets. She regularly posts scripture, as encouragement to others, on social media. Traci shared, "I have experienced a lot in life." She wants people to know that she is not defined by her circumstances or her medical diagnosis. Traci is defined by her identity in Christ alone. Traci is a daughter of our Most High King and continues to share Jesus through the encouragement and inspiration of her life story.

Isaiah 61:1-3

"The Spirit of the Lord God is upon me, because the Lord has anointed me to bring good news to the suffering and afflicted. He has sent me to comfort the brokenhearted, to announce liberty to captives, and to open the eyes of the blind. He has sent me to tell those who mourn that the time of God's favor to them has come, and the day of his wrath to their enemies. To all who mourn in Israel he will give: beauty for ashes; joy instead of mourning; praise instead of heaviness."

CHAPTER 10

FAITH & HEALING & RESTORATION

Jeanie M.

Jeanie is a very courageous woman of God who has endured great pain both physically and emotionally throughout her journey with Christ. Jeanie does not let her physical limitations cloud her vision for serving our most precious Lord, Jesus Christ. Her testimony is a true testament to her great courage, strength, and perseverance through Jesus. Jeanie opted for an in-person interview and gave me permission to record our session together. I had forwarded my "Jesus Questions" to her beforehand, so she was well prepared to share her responses with me. I have listened to our session together multiple times, taken notes, and hope and pray that I can bring justice to her beautiful story about the miracle of hope attained through Jesus.

Jesus has impacted Jeanie's life in a variety of ways. Knowing Him helps Jeanie not make sudden or impulsive decisions in life. She commented, "I may start watching a movie thinking it is a clean, solid movie, and then junk appears in it. I think, *oh no way I am not watching this!*" Jesus has helped Jeanie be more aware of our society and worldly things going on around her. There are many worldly influences and occurrences happening on a daily basis that Jeanie is sensitive to, and chooses to follow Jesus instead of the world.

She shared, "I almost died. There were preparations made for my funeral; however, God had a bigger and better plan for my life!" She started off seeing her doctor, who was a neurologist in the Twin Cities, and she did not know what more they could do for her. This doctor recommended her to the Mayo Clinic. Jeanie shared, "They took me to the clinic and one of my parents was with me at all times, either my mom or dad." At this time in Jeanie's life, she did not know the Lord; however, she realized later in life that Jesus never left her side, even before she knew Him. Jeanie tenderly commented, "He was not done with me yet!"

When Jeanie was twenty-nine years old, she suffered from a disabling condition. She was in the Mayo Clinic for six weeks. Jeanie shared, "I could not walk. I could not eat. I underwent all types of therapy: physical therapy, occupational therapy, and speech therapy. I had difficulty with cognitive tasks such as identifying objects on flash cards." The left side of her body weakened somewhat, like the effects of a stroke may have on someone; however, this was not a stroke. Jeanie's discharge paperwork from the Mayo Clinic showed she had the diagnosis of encephalopathy, most likely caused by a virus that attacked her brain. The source of this was undetermined by her team of doctors. Jeanie shared, "My brain was jumbled. I had a very good job as a Buyer, and I was unable to immediately return to work." She went to outpatient therapy for all types of therapy. Jeanie re-learned all types of life skills here again, commenting, "I learned how to write a check, cook in the kitchen... I was re-learning everything. I was twenty-nine years old. Yeah, that is probably the most painful thing I have ever gone through in my life!"

Jeanie was not a believer at this time in her life, so as she was going through this trial, she did not recognize He was there; however, today she can look back and see how Jesus was indeed there and has orchestrated absolutely everything in her life.

Jeanie recognizes that as a child of God, He will never leave her side. Jeanie shared, "I don't think I always relied on God before. In the last two years, I just feel... I can not do this on my own!" When she continues to experience trials, she recognizes that God has never left her side. "God has this! I am just happy to be alive! I can walk, and my brain is good!" She thinks that God is trying to teach her patience and to trust Him completely. Jeanie commented, "Whatever you have in store for me, God, I have accepted that. Your will be done." God has taught her a great deal in her life. Jeanie recalls a memory from her early twenties when she was in college. Jeanie and her friend would always see the handicapped bus near the large mall. She shared, "We chatted amongst ourselves and would say snide comments about them. I was a horrible, horrible person." She thought this was God teaching her and showing her humility in her life as she continues to walk through this trial today.

Jeanie commented, "I find so much good in people. They are so kind and go out of their way to help me. I just want to thank them. I want to be that person. Father, I want to be able to be that person!" God has taught Jeanie huge life lessons through this trial and struggle, that has changed her heart and made her into the courageous, kind, and empathic person that she is today. Jeanie shares, "I would have never been this person had I not come to this church, met the people that I have met... I would not be where I am today."

"Jesus is my everything! He is my Lord, my God, my Savior," Jeanie exclaimed through tears running down her face. She continued to explain, "I hope and pray that this is not the end of my story, and that God will heal me. My story is not over yet!" She tries to read and study the Bible every day, even if it may be only one verse, section, or paragraph. She shared, "I try to get my Bible reading each day, and we pray together now as a couple in the evening; something we did not used to do." Jeanie's biggest gift from the Lord is her love and ability to work with numbers. This is demonstrated in her full-time work and multiple side jobs. She commented, "Because of my physical limitations, this is my biggest gift I can share with the world."

Isaiah 41:10

"So do not fear, for I am with you; do not be dismayed, for I am your God. I will strengthen you and help you; I will uphold you with my righteous right hand."

Melody Evans

Melody is a strong and courageous woman, and she continues to demonstrate her inner strength and Godly character in her daily interactions with others. I have had the privilege to get to know Melody personally, and she has been a dear friend of mine for over a decade now. We have consoled one another through our losses and cheered each other on during our victories. I am excited that she was willing to share so openly about how Jesus has continually shown up and transformed her life. Melody opted to email her responses to my "Jesus Questions" to me, and she gave me permission to share her story in this book, using the responses she emailed back to me.

Jesus has given Melody the confidence to embrace who He created her to be, rather than her trying to meet the expectations of others. He remains the one unchanging constant in her life. He's been present through every transition and provides her with clear confirmations when she is on the right path. In Him, she finds unconditional love and acceptance, regardless of where she is at or what she is going through. Melody stated, "There is no checklist to earn His presence—His arms are always open, ready for me to ask for help." She continued to share that while some Christians doubted His work in her, she witnessed Him move in undeniable ways. Melody commented, "I don't need to defend it; I just let God speak for himself."

Perhaps the most painful experience Melody has had during her lifetime was losing her father, despite the fact that he was never emotionally supportive to her. After her father passed away two years ago, she began to realize just how deeply she had internalized his shaming and critical remarks over the past forty or so years. It became clear to her how harsh her inner voice had become, even to the point of criticizing something as simple as how she planted her garden. These past two years have been a journey of her distinguishing between God's gentle guidance and the lingering echoes of her father's perfectionist and shaming tendencies.

Jesus has always shown up in Melody's life, and she has always had a vibrant relationship with Him. When asked about how Jesus showed up in her life, Melody laughed and responded with, "How didn't he?" God has shown Himself to Melody through various Scripture passages, ACA (Adult Children of Alcoholics and Dysfunctional Families) readings, songs, conversations with friends, and witnessing that things do finally fall into place in her life after a lifetime of struggle. She repeatedly has found confirmation that she was on the right path. Melody shared, "This led to a deeper sense of healing and peace that I had ever experienced before." She went on to explain that her emotions no longer controlled her; instead, they serve as a guide to help her understand what is going on inside her.

The absence of a father figure during a difficult period of her mother's severe illness and passing had a profound effect on Melody emotionally. It nearly broke her, as she sought validation from external sources rather than from within her family. She commented, "When that failed, I felt shattered, believing I was beyond repair." However, God brought things into her life, and she began to discover her worth in being His creation, exactly how He intended her to be, rather than striving for the approval of others. This realization lifted a heavy burden from her heart.

God is Melody's source of peace and refuge, no matter the time or place. She trusts in His unwavering faithfulness, knowing that He has been by her side through every hardship. She commented, "I was never alone, and I never will be." She nurtures her relationship with Jesus by avoiding the urge to check her phone as soon as she wakes up. Melody sets aside quiet time with God first thing in the morning, before the distractions of the world begin, and she uses grounding techniques to stay mindful of God's presence. She strives to be her authentic self with everyone she encounters. Her routine includes prayer, meditation, listening to scripture while doing household tasks, journaling, and practicing daily affirmations that reinforce her identity in Christ and that she is worthy of love.

Melody has a very diverse skill set. She has a strong creative side, while also being highly organized. She excels at developing clear plans to move from Step A to Step B. Through her personal experiences, she has become both practical and deeply empathetic to those around her. She understands how to show compassion without enabling unhealthy behaviors. Additionally, she stated, "I am adept at reading non-verbal cues and understanding what is left unsaid."

Currently, her journey with the ACA Program (Adult Children of Alcoholics and Dysfunctional Families) has brought her to a place of being an ambassador of reconciliation, where she engages with individuals who have been hurt by the church—abuse that no pastor would endorse. Melody shared, "Many who would never step into a church are now coming to mine because they trust me for this weekly ACA Meeting." Remarkably, these same individuals play a significant role in her own healing process. She goes on to explain, "God is moving powerfully, even without Scripture being read or worship songs being sung. It's truly beautiful to witness God gently pursuing and softening hearts, no matter how small the steps may be."

As for Melody's employment, she finds herself at a crossroads right now. She would have previously mentioned Lakes Area Pregnancy Support, but that opportunity has recently come to an end. She commented, "I trust that God is orchestrating something that aligns even more closely with how He designed me. At the moment, I'm simply not in a position to clearly see what is next."

Hebrews 11:1

"Now faith is confidence in what we hope for and assurance about what we do not see."

Terri Kramer

Terri Kramer is a beautiful soul who loves our Lord with all her heart! She has overcome insurmountable odds when it comes to her health. Our families have been very close over multiple decades now, and she is a very close friend of mine as well. I am so pleased that she was willing to share so openly about the amazing miracle God performed in her life! Terri opted for an in-person interview and gave me permission to record our session together. I had forwarded my "Jesus Questions" to her beforehand, so she was well prepared to share her responses with me.

Terri feels like God has always been there for her since she was a little girl. When she attended Sunday School, she learned about Jesus and remembers specifically the song "This Little Light of Mine." She would sing this song as a testament to God to all the little neighbor kids as well. In High School, she got caught up in the drug scene when her family moved up to the Brainerd Lakes Area from Minneapolis. She started to skip school and use pot at that time, which led her to need a break from it all. She went into a hospital, and someone came out and presented Terri with a Bible, and the Pastor prayed over her. Terri shared, "I prayed that very night, and I felt the presence of Jesus with me." It took a couple of weeks to develop fellowship with other believers, who warmly took Terri in as family. She was later filled with the Spirit in Walker, MN, when an older couple discipled her. Terri commented, "I made up my mind that I was going to follow Jesus!" She was eighteen at this time, and Jesus has always been central to her life moving forward.

Terri goes on to explain that the most painful event that has ever occurred in her life, thus far, is definitely her experience with cancer. She shared, "It changed all of our lives so much, and I did not expect it as I was so healthy and all." The reason Terri went to the doctor in Crosby was that she started having abnormal bleeding. She just thought it was fibroids or something minor like that. This doctor had a biopsy done on Terri, and it came back as a diagnosis of cervical cancer. Terri shared, "As I was sitting in the office listening to my doctor tell me I have cancer, I just cried and cried. I just knew that this was going to be a long road." Her doctor told her that she could not treat her cancer since it had been there for a while. Terri was immediately referred to Minneapolis to receive more treatment. Dr. Judson scheduled surgery right away, and the lymph nodes looked clear after the surgery. Terri shared, "We were all thrilled. We thought it was all over, and I could go back to normal life again. Well, it has never been normal since."

A blessing came from God in the form of the $20,000 surgery that her father paid for upfront, and through the grant that Terri received later on. This grant reimbursed her father and paid for all medical bills moving forward with anything that had to do with her cancer. This was all God! Terri is so very thankful and appreciative of all the blessings God orchestrated during this extremely challenging period of time in her life. Terri shared, "My reprieve only lasted until a CT scan showed a large suspicious lymph node by my liver." They could not biopsy it without surgery, so she had a PET scan to see easily where the cancer was showing up. Terri had refused radiation even though her doctor urged her to do it. She and her husband, Jeff, felt that the risks far outweighed the benefits. In retrospect, her doctor told her it was a wise decision because the PET scan showed the cancer had already metastasized to the 4th stage in her para-aortic area, around the heart, and her liver.

They started chemotherapy right away, and a clinical trial that her doctor told them was so powerful that she had seen it completely knock the cancer out of coma patients. Terri commented, "I was scared. I did not want chemo!" It was a five to six-hour drive down to Hennepin University Hospital, and Jeff was with her the whole time. Also, their children came and expressed their love for her, and their love and faith in God. Terri shared, "It meant the world to me to have them close." Many friends and family members reached out with cards, letters, flowers, and prayers. They tried a barrage of "miracle cures" or alternative remedies to beat the cancer inside her. She comments, "I could not believe all that was out there!" She was almost through with the chemotherapy, and she developed mild Lymphedema in her left leg. Terri had been very proactive and had read everything she could get her hands on about cancer, so she knew all the signs to look for.

Terri finished the chemotherapy and got the PET results back, which showed that it had utterly failed! In fact, the cancer had grown! Her doctor could not believe it and wanted to start a whole other round of chemotherapy. Terri commented, "NO!!!" Terri had seen a program on Nightline called *A Good Death* about a woman who wrote about and researched death and dying. When this woman was diagnosed with pancreatic cancer, she and her husband decided to document it on film. She also refused more "treatment" when she got to the point that Terri was at. This woman advised taking time and spending it with your family at home instead of trying to chase a "cure" that may not even be successful.

They all agreed, no more chemotherapy; however, the diagnosis from her doctor, one year to live, was totally disheartening. Terri was completely devastated and placed herself in God's hands and said, "I trust you, Lord, whether I live or die. Just let my life glorify you!" God stayed so close to Terri through all of this. Terri shared, "I planned my funeral; however, I had even more people praying for me to live." A good friend started coming over once a week with lunch, and seven days' worth of the best kind of vitamins a person can get. Terri shared, "I am sure that helped!" The ladies from her church had a luncheon to "honor" her, and all she could do was cry the entire time she was there. They sang to our Lord, prayed, and even had a foot washing ceremony for her. Terri commented, "It was so moving and beautiful. Everyone shared their hearts and love." She was showered with cards, flowers, presents, notes, and a lovely luncheon. Terri even removed her wig and revealed to everyone her bald head. Terri shared, "Everyone got such a kick out of that, except my grandchildren." Terri and Jeff's children started having babies, and each time they would tell her, "You have to wait for this one now, Mom..." It honestly helped Terri keep her mind off her cancer to focus on her beautiful, blossoming family. She fell in love all over again with each child, and they made her want to live!

The lymphedema became unbearable, and every night, the pain would start by 6 p.m., and Jeff would do the lymphedema massage on her leg. Terri commented, "The pain in my left leg would become so excruciating that I thought I would pass out. Then, my meds would kick in, and it would crescendo off into a dispersion of pain, and I could finally fall asleep."

Some girlfriends of Terri's took her to see another one of their friends, Judy, who was battling cancer as well. She was not doing so well and had tried to fight her cancer "naturally" with juicing, coffee, enemas, and doctor visits to Tennessee. She had a whole room of devices, including a "Rife Machine," which Terri's grandfather had urged her to get for her own treatment. Terri shared, "People get so desperate that others start preying on that by selling them potions or 'that one thing' that is going to help them. Don't fall for it!" Judy tried them all and ended up doing chemotherapy in the end. She lost her hair, but grew many tumors on her neck, chest, and other areas on her body. In a few months, she passed away. Terri shared, "I decided that if there were going to be healing, it would have to be God!" During this period of time, many people encouraged her through Scripture, prayer, songs, and prophecy. Terri was so amazed at the love in God's people! She also began meeting up with her mom and sister regularly, three times a week. She looked forward to this time, as she could no longer drive and was forced to quit her job due to her illness with cancer.

One time around Christmas, Roger and Terry had a very special surprise waiting for her out in their truck. It was a huge tree full of beautiful handmade cards all tied with bows. These cards folded out with a very personal and uplifting message for Terri. They called it her "Blessing Tree," and it lit up with all her beautiful blessings on it. Terri shared, "One night when I was alone, I started reading all of them! I laughed and cried and was overwhelmed by the love of Jesus and His people!" For TEN years, Terri endured pain every single day until her MIRACLE of 2013 when the LORD healed her!!!

Terri had a CT scan because her hospice nurse could not believe how well she was doing. Her doctor called and said, "Well, either you had something, something else, or it's a MIRACLE! There is NO sign of it ANYWHERE!" Terri beamed and shared, "My lymphedema went away. My oxygen went from the 70s to the 90s. My bloodwork was normal. The pain went away, and I lost thirty-five pounds and gained back my energy!" Terri's doctor had previously diagnosed her cancer, in a PET scan, to have metastasized to the 4th stage in her para-aortic area, around the heart, and her liver. It was the worst case of cancer that she had ever seen, and in a letter to Heartland Hospice, she said, "In my opinion, this patient should not be alive!" Between 2010 and 2013, Terri lost 70 pounds, documented by both her doctor and her pharmacist.

God had other plans! Terri's friend, Donna, said, "You shall not die, but live and declare the works of the Lord." So, that is what Terri Kramer is doing for the rest of her life. Terri explains, "Don't put your trust in doctors, chemotherapy, potions, or anything else. Put your trust in God! He is our Healer! He loves us and paid a great price for you! Call on Him continually, and let His word be your food!" Terri can now rejoice with her children and seventeen grandchildren. Praise the Lord! Today, Terri encourages others through sharing her story, loving people, and sharing the goodness and glory of our Lord, Jesus Christ, with others!

Psalm 73:23-26

"Yet I am always with you; you hold me by my right hand. You guide me with your counsel, and afterward you will take me into glory. Whom have I in Heaven but you? And earth has nothing I desire besides you. My flesh and my heart may fail, but God is the strength of my heart and my portion forever."

Tracy McNamara

Tracy McNamara is truly a confident and courageous woman of God, and she has a story that will melt your heart. Tracy opted for a phone interview and gave me permission to record our session together. I had forwarded my "Jesus Questions" to her beforehand, so she was well prepared to share her responses with me. I have listened to our session together multiple times, taken notes, and hope and pray that I can bring justice to her beautiful life story.

She started by stating that Jesus most impacted her life through the idea that He has made sure that she is aware that she is still worthy of His love, and that His reassurance is her reassurance. Somewhere in 2013, she did not quite feel right and had difficulty putting a finger on what was wrong. She began having conversations with herself about this uneasy feeling she was having in the pit of her stomach. There were challenges in her marriage at this time, and she was in a pretty dark place. She told herself that if she ever got cancer, she would not do anything about it and she would just let it go, allowing herself out of the current predicament that she was in. She had decided to not go to the doctor and see why she was not feeling well. She was working with some nurses in October, and one of the nurses told her, "Don't borrow trouble or claim any bad feelings about yourself." Tracy continued to ignore it, and at the end of December, she was talking to a different set of nurses that she worked with and explained to them how she felt full a lot, and was going to the bathroom quite frequently. Those nurses told her that she needed to get in and see a doctor about all this. She wondered what type of doctor she should see about this and decided upon her woman doctor and OBGYN for a starting place.

Tracy was very nervous at this time and questioned whether or not she really wanted to know what was going on with her. She made the appointment and ended up seeing a PA that she had never seen before. This doctor told Tracy that she was about fifteen weeks pregnant. Tracy laughed and told the PA that eight years prior to this, she had had an ablation and never had another cycle following that. Tracy laughed again and said, "That ain't happening." She continued to explain to her doctor that something just did not feel right down there. She could actually cup in her hand, whatever it was, and hold it. That doctor insisted that she was about fifteen weeks pregnant. Tracy told her, "There is no possible way that I can be pregnant due to the ablation done to her in the past." Tracy took two pregnancy tests and both came out negative, so they sent her to another place in town for imaging and further diagnosis of her current condition. They did an exterior ultrasound on Tracy, and she began to become nervous as they started measuring things. This was followed by a vaginal ultrasound. Once again, the nurse started taking measurements, adding to the anxiety Tracy was already feeling at that time. While this was taking place, Tracy started having conversations with God and bargaining with Him, "If this is not this God, I will be a better person..." This was immediately followed by a breast mammogram exam. While she was having this portion of the exam done, the nurse came in and told her that the doctor wanted to see her back in his office. Tracy had come to the hospital all by herself, so this all did not truly hit her until she got back out to her car. She called her mom, and her mother met her at Allen Hospital. After her mom arrived, they took Tracy away to the back of the hospital, and they both sat waiting for about twenty minutes before the doctor came to see her. The next thing Tracy heard from that doctor was, "You have a tumor and we are sending you to Iowa City." At this point, all Tracy could do was cry. Tracy began screaming and telling her doctor that it was too late and that she had waited too long. They called her on the phone and let her know the appointment date for Iowa City, and that she would be seeing Dr. Bender. The appointment originally had been made for the end of that month, and this news did not go over well with her. Tracy became unhinged at that point, stating, "I have a tumor in me and you want me to wait?"

Tracy went home and tried to return to life as usual, and about a week later, she got a call from Iowa City saying that they would be able to see her sooner. They were able to see her within two days of that second call. She told her husband about the appointment, and at that time, he was not worried at all. Previously, about a year ago, Tracy's mom had a tumor, which was benign, not cancerous, removed from her body. Then Tracy and her husband, Chad, went down there, and her mom accompanied them to Iowa City. The doctors decided that they wanted to do all their own testing on Tracy, so she had to repeat the same tests that were previously done on her. They also performed a CT scan on her. They proceeded to examine her, and in the process, must have exacerbated her tumor, because she had extreme pain in her stomach region that needed to be subdued. Upon the results of all the medical tests they did on Tracy, her doctor stated, "It has to come out," and made an appointment for her a month later. Once again, Tracy questioned, "You are going to make me wait a month?" Two days later, they called her and told her they had an opening that Wednesday to remove her tumor. This was truly a God thing on both occasions that Tracy was able to get into the hospital right away for her appointment and her tumor surgery.

Tracy went to Iowa City that Wednesday and had the surgery done, including having a total hysterectomy. At this time, Tracy said to God, "If this is cancer, you will have to put a smoking patch on me because I will never smoke again in my life." She has never smoked again, to this day, for ten years. Friday at noon, she had her surgery, and her mom stayed overnight with her in the hospital. The surgery was at noon, and by 9 p.m., she was up, walking the hospital halls with her mother. The nurses were blown away by Tracy's commitment and perseverance to begin walking again. They had told her she could just dangle her legs; however, Tracy did not want to do just that. She told them, "I want to stand up and walk." Tracy was placed with a very combative roommate, so after pleading with them profusely, they did move Tracy to a private room of her own. Tracy and her mom kept walking every day through the long halls of the hospital. They notified Tracy that she could return home on Monday. She and her mom were walking at about noon on Sunday, and Tracy stopped abruptly, and all of a sudden, she could not walk anymore. Tracy asked her mom to please go get help, while leaving her to sit on a bench to wait. They came down right away and brought Tracy back to her bed. After that, she was not able to pass gas or have a bowel movement. A suppository, enema, and reverse osmosis were all used with no positive results. She stated, "My belly hurt so bad it felt like it was going to explode." They did not want to release her from the hospital until she, at the very least, passed gas or had a bowel movement.

Tracy woke up the next morning to twenty-five student interns in her room and her doctor. Tracy told her doctor, "This is barbaric, I told you I was unable to go to the bathroom for eight days when I got here and five days since, so I am on day thirteen not going." Tracy then had an X-ray done that showed that she had an alias, so she could not go home yet.

They dissected her tumor to determine what kind and stage of cancer she had at that time. Tracy told me that she looked seven and a half to eight months pregnant when she first came into the hospital. The process of figuring out what kind and stage of cancer she had takes about seven days. She was required to stay at the hospital until she could go to the bathroom normally, or pass enough gas that they approved her release. Her mother stayed in that hospital room with her for moral support. Tracy knew that she was going to receive her results the very next day, and she pleaded her case with God. As she was trying to close her eyes and go to sleep, she saw a bright colored kaleidoscope going on in her head, and this was a little scary for Tracy as it was spinning at a fast pace. It slowed down eventually and focused on what Tracy was supposed to pay attention to or look at. She opened her eyes and stated, "In the name of Jesus Christ, go away!" Then she closed her eyes again, and the image had gotten very close and formulated into a distinguishable shape; it was Jesus. She was able to see the side of his body and face as she watched Him intently. Tracy shared with me, "Jesus looked up at God and then He put His head back down, closed His eyes, and He prayed for me." She found extreme comfort in this very tender moment with Jesus. The next day, the doctor came in and told her, "We found you at Stage 1A, where less than fifteen percent of women with ovarian cancer are found." Her doctor told her she had a mix of two different kinds of ovarian cancer. Tracy told me that she could not tell me what stage her cancer was at before her divine incident with Jesus; however, after that meeting with Jesus during the night, she was Stage 1A. Prior to that incident, her tumor was bigger than a saucer for a teacup. She shared with me, "I felt great, and He just did so much work for me; He changed my life and made me better!" Tracy said that He was giving her more opportunities to spread the Word.

Tracy got sick after her first session of chemotherapy. She had a staph infection in her stomach, so she had to return to Iowa City. Her first roommate came in at about 2 a.m., and it was very dark in the room. She was able to hear them wheeling somebody into the room, and Tracy greeted her new roommate. When she woke up the next morning, her new roommate and her mother were gone. Tracy's roommate (Brandy) had to have an amputation after her ovarian cancer had metastasized to her breast. After she returned from her surgery, Tracy, her roommate, and her mom talked about a variety of different things. Tracy's roommate had gone nine months prior to them figuring out that she had ovarian cancer. When they opened up and diagnosed her roommate at nine months, she was a Stage 4C cancer patient. Five months later, Tracy's former roommate did pass away. Tracy commented to me, "I wondered sometimes if I should have died as well." Clearly, this was a miracle, and Jesus saved her. There are people out there who need to know both Tracy's and Brandy's stories today.

Tracy wants to encourage women to advocate for themselves and get a second or third medical opinion: "Don't let people ignore the importance of identifying and detecting cancer early. Have perseverance in the process of figuring out what is wrong and how to correct it. Be proactive and not reactive when it comes to ovarian cancer or any other type of cancer out there. You are somebody's mother, sister, daughter, wife, and grandmother. Most importantly, you are a daughter of the Most High King."

Tracy was encouraged through God's words, "Be still and know that I am God." This meant that she needed to trust God and be one hundred percent reliant upon Him. She stated, "I don't know where my cancer was before my encounter with Him." However, I know He worked in my life when I had that encounter with Him, and the next day I was a stage 1A when everything would have pointed to me being a Stage 4C. This means that her cancer was still in its capsule and infancy stage, and had not broken into other areas of her body.

Today, Tracy has a vibrant relationship with Jesus. She trusts Him and knows that she can always go to Him with anything in her life. She shared with me, "I know that I can always go to God in prayer, and He might not give me the answer that I want, but He will always be there for me and love me unconditionally. The answer God provides will always be the right one for me." The way Tracy nurtures her relationship with Jesus is through little prayers here and there all day. She cherishes her little conversations with Jesus every day. The gifting Tracy has from the Lord is sharing with women that they need to listen to their bodies. She reminds them of her and Brandy's story whenever she is given the opportunity to do so. She talks to everyone about this topic, and wants to help women be detected early and be survivors with ovarian cancer and other forms of cancer as well.

As I sat and listened to Tracy Steen's story of how Jesus has shown up and works in her life, tears began to swell in my eyes. You see, Tracy has been a dear friend of mine since high school and beyond. Our family went to see her in Waterloo, IA, after her ovarian cancer surgery, and I had prayed many prayers of healing and restoration over my friend, as I am sure many others did as well. Her story is clearly an example of how God used something negative in her life and turned it around for good.

Psalm 46:10

"Be still, and know that I am God; I will be exalted among the nations, I will be exalted in the earth."

CHAPTER 11

FAITH & HOPE & PRAYER

Ann L.

Ann has a strong faith in Jesus Christ and has been raised with the church since she was a young child. Jesus is her Rock, and she enjoys sharing about Him at every opportunity she is given in life. Ann opted to email her responses to my "Jesus Questions" to me, and she gave me permission to share her story in this book, using the responses she emailed back to me.

Jesus has most impacted Ann's life in a number of different ways. He has given her great confidence that she is loved, belongs to Him, and is fully and unconditionally accepted by Jesus Christ. She does not have to fear death, knowing that Jesus saved her and has given her eternal and everlasting life. Jesus has given Ann the confidence that all things that happen in her life happen for a reason, including the difficult things and hard events. She understands that God is working all things for her good and His glory.

One of the most painful incidents Ann has gone through is happening currently in her life. This is raw and fresh in her heart right now, and it has been a very difficult season for her to endure. She is currently pregnant, and it has been a very challenging and fearful time for her. She started off with extreme nausea and vomiting in the first trimester of her pregnancy. She had difficulty sleeping and waking up in the middle of the night. This, coupled with her heart pounding, has led to insomnia. She has also recently been diagnosed with gestational diabetes. The combination of all of these things has caused her to have fear for the health of her baby, and for herself as she struggles with feeling unwell and unhealthy right now.

Jesus has come and shown up in a mighty way in her life right now. He ministers to her through the Bible and brings her reassurance in her current circumstances with her pregnancy. Jesus has comforted her heart during this time, and continues to do so during this particularly trying season of her life. He makes the Bible come alive and directs her to various verses of comfort while speaking directly to her about her current situation. Friends and family continue to send uplifting Bible verses and messages that have brought Ann comfort during this time. Many have been praying for Ann and the safety of her and her baby. The Lord has also loved Ann through the tender care of her husband. A verse that has meant a lot to her during this season is Isaiah 40:11, "He will tend his flock like a shepherd; he will gather the lambs in his arms; he will carry them in his blossom, and gently lead those that are with young."

Through this difficult pregnancy, this path she never would have chosen herself, the Lord has turned into good by using it to quiet her heart, have her rest in Him, allow Him to love her, and learn to trust her body and baby to Him. Ann said, "I've heard that motherhood is all about letting go, so this is good practice for me." She also commented on the new ways that she has learned to be healthier through eating nourishing foods for herself and their baby.

Ann's relationship today with Jesus is her anchor and the mainstay of her life. She continues to keep Jesus in the center of her life on a multitude of different levels. Jesus is her joy, comfort, and confidence, and everything flows out of Him. She nurtures this relationship with Jesus through her daily readings of a section of the Bible. She told me that she doesn't just read it, but she slows down and truly meditates on the words she is reading in the Bible. She also makes the effort to see how these verses directly apply to her life. Along with that Bible reading, she also prays and worships our Lord in various ways throughout the day.

Our Lord has given her a heart of compassion for the hurting and a passion for praying for them. She shared with me that many people have told her that the cards and letters she has written to them have blessed and encouraged them during various trials in their lives. Ann said, "It seems the Lord has given me the gift of encouragement through letter writing." And that amazes her. Ann will continue to reach out to those who are hurting and in need, and also disciple others through God's word. She loves writing cards to people and enjoys visiting with those who need a friend. Along with that, she also enjoys praying and interceding for others on their behalf. She said, "There are so many opportunities to serve the Lord and others if we just let Him lead us!"

John 12:26

"If anyone serves me, he must follow me; and where I am, my servant will be as well. If anyone serves me, the Father will honor him."

Heather Robinson

Heather has a heart of gold and a precious heart for the Lord today. She has had a difficult and powerful testimony of how she got there. I have had the privilege to personally get to know Heather over the years since junior high school. It is later in life, over the last decade or so, that we have reconnected as friends and shared what is going on in each other's lives. I am excited that she was willing to share so rawly and transparently about how Jesus has continually shown up and transformed her life. She is a true inspiration and source of divine encouragement to others today. Heather opted to email her responses to my "Jesus Questions" to me, and she gave me permission to share her story in this book, using the responses she emailed back to me.

Jesus has impacted Heather's life on a multitude of different levels. Heather shares, "I was born into sin; however, I did not come to this realization until later in life, growing up in a nominal Christian Lutheran Church." She goes on to explain that she always had a reverence for God and understood that He was up there and she was down here. Her parents had major feuds as Heather was growing up, and she looked to her older brother and tried to emulate his behavior as the proper example in the household. Heather was very shy, and everyone was always telling her that she was a nice and good girl. Heather commented, "I knew deep inside that I was not a nice girl at all, even though adults continued to admire this quality in me." Heather knew she was a bad child. She did not commit any major sins; however, she did not respect or treat her mother kindly at all. She developed deviant thought and behavior patterns. She would take out all her anger and disobey her mother regularly. Her mother would get exasperated with her and get out the yardstick. Heather shared, "I knew I was wrong, and yet I would push my mother to exasperation to use it on me." When Heather was in her twenties, her mother shared with her, "Heather, I would spank you and spank you, and your response was to not change your current behavior. Your response was to hide the yardstick."

When Heather discussed her disobedience, God protected her in each of those rebellious times. Heather explained, "At the root of it was that I thought I had to solve my own problem and hence I leaned on my own understanding." She was trying to make her own path in life. Heather needed no one but herself at that time in her life. It began when she was a child with a quest for power and self-sufficiency. Heather commented, "The men I was involved with were my allegiance for attaining self-sufficiency." She leaned on her own understanding instead of asking for God's help. Heather shared, "I knew fully that I was dealing with the wrong people; however, I wanted to show them Jesus." Heather explained that at the root of her rebellion was hubris, or excessive pride and self-confidence.

During Heather's adolescent years, Heather went through a crisis period of time when her brother left for college. Her friends from junior high were not her friends in high school, and Heather found herself alone. Then, a new neighbor moved into their mainly elderly neighborhood, and things started to look up for her. This new neighbor, Ann, was going to purchase Heather's goat from her, and introduced themselves to her parents to make the arrangements to buy the goat. This new neighbor also had a Bible study and invited her neighborhood to come to her home for this Bible study. She had two sons who were younger than her, and she got to know both of Heather's parents well. Heather's new neighbor invited Heather to go to her church with her. Heather began to confide her thoughts and concerns in Ann. She felt comfortable talking with Ann, as her parents were much older and their responses matched an audience of a different decade. Ann's church seemed to be alive, and they used charismatic expression; her parents' church seemed dull to her at that time. Ann shared Scripture with Heather and inserted her name into it, which became Heather's favorite song today, Psalm 117. Heather learned that she was formed in her mother's womb and deeply meditated on John 3:16. This is where she learned that Jesus died for her sins.

One summer night in July of 1987, Heather watched a special on television that changed her life forever. It was a drama about a young college woman who had forsaken her life in America to serve others in Central America. She assisted people there and was killed for driving people to safety. The actress playing this part was Melissa Gilbert, and they depicted her in an ethereal, cloudy heaven after she died. She recited the "Footprints" in the sand poem. Heather had never heard that poem before. Heather commented, "It was then that I realized that Jesus carried me and bore my sins." She went outside on that crystal clear summer night, and the stars were shining like black diamonds. Heather cried out to God, "Take my life! I am making a wreck of mine!" It was in that moment that Heather realized that God was no longer up there; Jesus was here with her. She asked Him to save her. The beauty in this lonely, turbulent scenario is that God was not only working in her life.

Heather shared, "The sin I gave to Jesus was the same sin that my mom had as well." Her mother felt that she could not give her daughter enough, because Heather would not change her disrespect toward her. Her mother realized that she needed Jesus, too.

Heather emotionally shared, "The worst thing that occurred in my life was watching and knowing a friend who died without Jesus Christ." This was the worst feeling of knowing that she could have been there for them, or she could have done more to help, instead of leaving them to their own devices. Heather shared, "I know that all I can do is glorify God for saving me, and hope that His words convict other lost souls. I lean on Him and ask Jesus to lead me."

Heather commented, "The most painful moments that I have gone through in life are too numerous to list; it is hard to pick one most painful moment." Heather recalled several times she disobeyed God and did things in her own strength instead of relying on the Lord. She chose boyfriends who were not Christian. She had incorrect thinking of who she was and did not fully grasp her identity in Christ yet at this time in her life. Media influences glamorize one-night stands, and thought patterns that men would never choose her as their forever love; she would always stand on the back burner as they chose another before her. Heather commented, "These were all lies of Satan."

These subtle thoughts—"little foxes"—are mainstreamed into current culture. Later, these same thoughts would manifest themselves into sexual assault, rape, emotional adultery, controlling relationships, and illegitimate marriages. The mind is a battlefield, and sure enough, the moment you utter the battle, it will be directly followed by a test from Satan. Heather compartmentalized things, and she took the Lord for granted. Heather shared, "I knew what occurred was wrong, but there were times I did not know how to get out of those situations. The Lord protected me even though I was in rebellion in some of those situations." She deceived herself into believing that those things were all right. Later, she confessed all those things to the Lord and asked Him to remove these sins from her; He did.

Heather shared openly about her past in hopes that other people would not fall prey to these idols. She believed that the main issues she had were hubris, excessive pride, or self-confidence. She believed that she could do it all on her own and that she did not need God or a man in her life. She thought she had to solve all things on her own, when in fact she could not. Heather shares, "Every day we battle struggles, but Jesus has overcome the world. He has removed all of these sins from me." Heather goes on to explain that she praises God for taking away those thoughts of sin.

Today, Heather clings to Jesus every day. She reads His Word and asks Him, "What do you want me to know and learn?" She believes that between Praise and Prayer that there is Life. Heather explains, "This is the life I was meant to have, which God created me to live out." She attends multiple church events because that is where people who love Him go to socialize. Heather deals with a lot of criticism as she has developed a critical spirit. Heather shared, "I now choose to give Jesus my faults. I ask Jesus to save me. He is my savior every day!" She also listens to Christian radio programs to help feed her soul.

Heather is unsure of her talents and giving from the Lord; however, she believes it is important to discover your spiritual gifts from the Lord. She attended Theophostic Counseling, where the counselor asked the Holy

Spirit to reveal what was hindering her. She did that with them, and the counselor asked her to give her sins to the Lord. Heather commented, "I can't because no one should have to bear what I did." This was the moment that Heather realized she was holding back and choosing not to obey Jesus by giving Him all those ugly things from her past and laying them at His feet. The irony here is that God already knows everything in the first place before, during, and after it happens in your life. You can not hide anything from God!

Romans 10:9

"If you declare with your mouth, Jesus is Lord, and believe in your heart that God raised him from the dead, you will be saved."

Michelle Y.

Michelle has a very tender heart for the Lord, and her love for Jesus and others shines through in her interactions with others. Michelle opted for an in-person interview and gave me permission to record our session together. I had forwarded my "Jesus Questions" to her beforehand, so she was well prepared to share her responses with me. I have listened to our session together multiple times, taken notes, and hope and pray that I can bring justice to her beautiful story about the miracle of life.

Michelle was raised Catholic up until the second grade, learning about God through her grandparents, and then attended church occasionally for weddings and funerals. It was not until she turned fifteen, while dating the man who would become her husband, that she started attending his church with him and his family. Michelle shared, "It was at this time that I started learning more about God and Jesus, and building a relationship with Him."

At one point and time, Michelle questioned whether or not she and her husband would ever be able to become parents. Today, she and her husband are the proud parents of three children, two girls and one boy. How did they get there? Michelle was told by doctors that the probability of her becoming pregnant was very slim due to having poor-quality eggs. On a rating scale of A to D, she had mostly B and C eggs. Their final attempt to have children was in vitro fertilization (IVF), and they did that two times; the first time failed, but they got pregnant the second time. They were able to retrieve three eggs to be stored for later use. They were able to get pregnant, and everything was great during the pregnancy up to about twenty-nine weeks. She had started spotting and went to see her doctor right away. Everything seemed to be progressing normally, so they did not think anything was wrong with the baby. She returned to her doctor for her next scheduled appointment and let him know that she was continuing to have spotting. Her doctor advised that they take a second look at her and discovered that she was beginning to dilate. He immediately put Michelle on bed rest. Michelle commented, "I still had my strong faith and trust in the Lord." She somehow knew that everything was going to be all right. Their first child came early at ten weeks' premature due to kidney stones. Michelle was put on bed rest for five days after spotting. One morning, she woke up in extreme pain and went to the emergency room, where they admitted her and waited for her doctor to come and examine her. He told Michelle that she needed to pass the stones naturally, as they could not do anything because of how far along she was in her pregnancy. They would not be able to do a stent to help the stones pass, and she would have to pass the stones on her own. She was admitted to the hospital on a Sunday night, and by Wednesday, the stones had passed. She anticipated returning home on Thursday; however, this did not happen. The pain and contractions got worse throughout the night, and the next morning, she had dilated to a level six overnight. The entire time, she did not worry, and she knew God had this. Michelle commented, "I was not concerned, and I knew my baby was healthy." They had given her steroids for her baby's lungs to develop, and they told her nothing was wrong with her except that her baby was small. Friday morning, her doctor came in and told her that she was going to have her baby; however, he just did not know when. He had decided that he was going to come back and see Michelle at about noon that day. As he was in the middle of talking about the potential of what early labor would be, he started talking to the nurses and giving them specific instructions to follow. Michelle shared, "I was concerned and confused; I did not know anything or understand what was happening around me." They proceeded to unhook Michelle from her IVs on the wall, and she inquired about what was going on. Her doctor shared with her, "You are going into preterm labor, and we need to do an emergency C-Section now or your baby will not make it." Michelle's baby's heart rate dropped to sixty, and Michelle could see her husband crying on the other side of the room, as they were wheeling Michelle off to surgery. Michelle told her husband, "It's going to be okay; everything is going to be fine, God's got this." Michelle woke up four hours later and saw her baby for the first time. She was three pounds and 5.6 ounces and was in the Neonatal Intensive Care Unit (NICU) for six weeks and a day. Michelle's original due date was February 23rd. The doctors and nurses told her that she would be able to go home with her baby around that time. Michelle's baby was amazing and had no complications whatsoever, and she was not placed on oxygen at all. She was only under bilirubin lights for about a day. Michelle shared, "Everything was just a miracle as God was working through us and through our baby, knowing all the complications that could have happened with having preterm labor did not happen." Their baby passed every single milestone quickly, and they said originally she would come home around her original due date of February 23rd. Later, they predicted that she would be able to go home by Valentine's Day, and she did so well that she was able to come home on February 29th. This was truly a miracle in itself.

They miraculously got pregnant again with their second child while their first child was about ten months old. They were able to get pregnant naturally without IVF and were so very thankful to God for this tremendous blessing in their lives. Michelle commented, "My husband told me later that he prayed so hard that God would bless them with more children." Michelle's husband was so happy that God blessed them with more children that he wanted to give that child a biblical name. The couple researched God's baby names and came up with a name that means *God has answered*. Michelle stated, "My husband helped me keep the faith in the difficult times. His continuous prayer, leading our family, and not giving up encouraged me to be strong."

Michelle and her husband had two children, and her faith was beginning to grow, learning more and more about the Lord. Three years went by, and they still did not have another baby, so they decided to try to use the three eggs that they had stored through their previous experience of IVF. None of these three eggs worked when they were implanted. Miraculously, they got pregnant again on their own. This time, they lost the baby to a miscarriage. Three months after that, they got pregnant with their son, who was their third and last child.

They left the church where they were at when their baby was a couple of months old, and her husband led them to their home church for about a year and a half. When their third child was about eighteen months old, they decided that they needed to get back into a church body and fellowship with other believers. Michelle did Google searches on different churches and showed them to her husband. He looked at their mission statements and read what they represented, and he was unsatisfied with what they would provide for his family. They found their current church after her husband guided them toward it. Michelle commented, "After the very first sermon, they were hooked. We knew this was our home. This was where we needed to be. This church has grown my faith and my desire to have God and Jesus in my life more and more and more." She tells people that she didn't really know anything until she started coming to this specific church. She went on to explain that she started reading the Bible and started learning more about Jesus, and everything He had done for us. Michelle shares, "I started learning about everything Jesus has done for me in my life." Through the love of their children, God showed Michelle all the miraculous things He can do. She commented, "Listening to different sermons, and the Bible studies, getting to know everyone at church, and the elders and pastoral staff; they just filled my cup. They filled my cup!" Michelle finally realized that this is where she needed to be, and it was working for her and her family. This church gave her the desire to learn more about Jesus, and she dug into the Bible for the first time in her life. She continued to notice little things that God did for her in her life. They were having financial difficulties, and randomly, they would get a check in the mail or a rebate for something. God helped provide them with gas money, food, and placed wonderful people in their lives, who understood the struggles they had, who provided them with blessings as well. The church itself helped them as well. Michelle shared, "All these wonderful blessings in Jesus' name came to us!" Michelle explained that she never had a born-again moment; however, she was sitting in church, and all of a sudden, she just felt different, and she felt the Holy Spirit in her body. Michelle shared, "This has just changed." She was inspired by the movie *God's Not Dead,* and it encouraged her to dig deeper into the Bible and know God more. Michelle stated, "This movie gave me goosebumps and the hope and the will to keep living after having four years of infertility."

Two painful incidents Michelle shared about during her life were the passing of her grandmother, who taught her all about Jesus, and the struggles she had with infertility. Her grandmother was her hero and mentor. She went through some very dark days during this time when she knew she wanted to be a mom and was not able to be. Michelle had a suicide attempt on her life, and by God's divine intervention, it did not happen, and Michelle is alive today to share about how amazing God is. There was a phone call Michelle received at the exact moment she was going to end her life. She realized that God was telling her, "No! This is not going to happen." Michelle goes on to explain that Jesus helped her realize that she needed to live, that she was destined for more at that time, that her work was not done; it was not finished. That phone call, through God, saved her life!

Michelle describes her relationship with Jesus today as the BEST thing she has ever had in her life! God gives her signs that He is there when she is struggling. When Michelle is having a bad day, out of nowhere, there is a song on the radio, text, or phone call from a friend right at that exact moment that she needs to hear. Michelle shared, "That is God. I look up and I say, 'Thank you, Jesus!'" She prays multiple times a day for herself, her job, her coworkers, family, friends, and church family. She sends text messages, as well as encouragement to others. She leads her children in prayer, reads the Bible with Scripture daily, and engages in a phone devotional daily. The gift that God has blessed Michelle with is being a mom and giving her the strength to keep going every single day, even when she is feeling hopeless in her darkest times. Michelle struggles with a lot of medical issues, and God encourages her on a daily basis. God helps her keep moving and going through very difficult times at work and helps her in a physical and emotional capacity daily. He gives her strength in financial and parenting difficulties. Michelle shares her story with anybody who is struggling with something similar to something she has struggled with in the past; she reaches out to them and encourages them. She has worked with the most difficult types of population there is: women who are chemically dependent, women who gave birth to positive babies, children with disabilities caused by alcoholism, and children with autism. Michelle closes with this comment, "I go to them, I reach out to them. I share my story. I share the hope I have in Christ. I let them know that they are not alone. The impossible is possible with God!"

Matthew 19:26

"With man this is impossible, but with God all things are possible."

Sara Otremba

Sara Otremba is a very courageous and resilient woman of God. We see in her testimony story how God shows up and orchestrates perfectly, in His timing and His way, all the beautiful details in her life. She and her husband, Zak, have been blessed beyond measure, and this is her story of how they overcame the "ten years of tears" and gave birth to their sweet little miracle, their daughter Kylie Joy. Sara opted for an in-person interview and gave me permission to record our session together. I had forwarded my "Jesus Questions" to her beforehand, so she was well prepared to share her responses with me. I hope and pray that I can bring justice to her beautiful story about the miracle of life.

Jesus showed up early in Sara's life as she was saved at a very young age. Sara shares, "Everything else He has done on top of that is icing on the cake." She grew up in a Christian home where the Gospel was taught regularly, and life was fairly simple. Life was not close to perfect; however, she did have a foundation of married parents who aspired to model Jesus Christ in the center of their lives. She went to church two times a week, the children did chores, and Sara shared a room with her siblings growing up. Sara went to college and met and fell in love with Zak, her husband. Sara reflected, "A lot of Christians saved at a young age, who were granted the gift of growing up like I did, think they don't have a great testimony of salvation. However, what a mercy it is that God spared me from going down a hard life of suffering big consequences before falling in love with Him." Sara attributes her dad for helping her see that point of view. Sara shared, "I want to be clear that it doesn't mean life growing up was always easy and I never struggled with interpersonal relationships, but that is another story altogether." God made the Gospel very clear to Sara and caused her heart to love that truth and seek Jesus from the early age of six years old.

The most painful incident that Sara ever experienced in her life, spoken in her words, is, "I've yet to be able to process the most painful experience. I am still waiting through that one, and anticipating God at work while I wait to get to the other side, whether now or in eternity." One of the most difficult things God has ordained Sara to endure is waiting to have children. Sara commented, "For as long as I remember, my dream in life was to get married young and become a stay-at-home mom soon after. The thought never crossed my mind that it would be an issue." Sara's perspective was that almost every lady she knew, who wanted children, got them right away. When she got married at the young age of nineteen, after only knowing her husband for six months, things were looking pretty good for her in that area. Sara shared, "Step one was done. Now for step two... little did I know the long journey we had ahead of us." After eight years of tears and prayers, and trying desperately to have children, they had some fertility testing done. The results revealed that it was going to be nearly impossible for them to conceive, outside of spending a lot of money on medical intervention. Even that was not guaranteed to be successful, so they gave up trying and accepted their lot in life.

Sara shared, "Although it was hard to accept that my biggest dream would never come true, it ended up being a very healthy thing for me to struggle with." Like a butterfly that breaks out of its cocoon prematurely and never fully develops healthy wings for flight, Sara was also in a healthy waiting period, too, as God was teaching and instructing her in various areas of her life. Sara shared, "Through the years of trying and being unsuccessful, God was breaking down my pride. I thought I somehow deserved children because I did all the right things." Sara went on to explain that she was a good Christian girl who didn't involve herself sexually until after she was married. This was something that very few people around her had done. None of them seemed to be having an issue bearing children. Sara shared, "Surely I wouldn't either. However, I grew to realize that no matter who we are or what we have or have not done, none of us is more deserving than anyone else to receive any mercy from God." Sara realized that her sin, although different from the one she was focusing on around her, was just as bad in God's eyes. She commented, "I am no better or more holy... Therefore, my standing outside of God's saving grace is the same. Condemned. Even to take pride in my salvation is wrong because I didn't achieve that myself. Only by God's sovereign will did He choose me, not because my life or heart convinced Him that I earned His favor." Sara explained that the encouragement was in the fact that God had a big picture plan. She shared, "He was not merely concerned for my temporary desires, but for the overall well-being of my soul." After a few years of giving up on the idea of children, they found out she was pregnant.

Sara shared tenderly, "I am so thankful that God showed mercy on my daughter by not giving the 'old' me to her as her mom. Of course, nobody will be perfect until eternity, but the mom I am now is a much better version than she would have gotten eleven years before." Not just in the area of motherhood was God working; He was also working with Sara in the area of her becoming a better wife to her husband. This, in turn, would help them become better parents to their daughter. Sara shared, "God used those childless years to really prune and strengthen mine and my husband's marriage." There was one other huge encouragement to both Sara and Zak when they got pregnant. Sara commented, "When we started telling people I was pregnant, we had many people tell us that they never stopped praying for a miracle. I was overwhelmed by the number of people that told us that, and from people I wouldn't expect would take the time to pray for what we thought was a lost cause."

Sara shared how Jesus turned around their potentially negative situation for good: "Not only in my spiritual life was that time (ten years of tears) not wasted, but also in the practical things of life." Sara jumped right into service at her church with the Children's Ministry after they got married. This was something that she did not know if she would have committed herself so heavily to if they had their own children to care for. Sara commented, "Thankfully, I'm able to stay in the High School Ministry today, though I have stepped back a little." Sara and Zak were able to pay off her student loans and their car loan at that time as well. God was working in their finances to help them prepare for this new little one's arrival. Sara shared, "I tend to get in a tizzy about finances fairly easily, and we had many ups and downs. I was thankful that God, in His mercy, provided the opportunity for us to pay off our student loans before getting pregnant."

Today, Sara has a vibrant relationship with our Lord. She is able to look back on God's faithfulness and His wisdom in this circumstance to give her peace and comfort in the current situations she would like to change. Sara commented, "It reminds me that God is good, wise, He does care, His decisions are always right, and that temporary things are not what really matter." Sara goes on to explain, "Now I wish I could say this means I never worry or complain, or doubt... but that's not the case." She finds comfort in two Bible verses: 1) Romans 5:2-6 and 2) James 1:2-4. Sara can testify to having more endurance, better character, and stronger hope now than before their "ten years of tears." Romans 5:2-6 says, "Through Him (Jesus) we have also obtained access by faith into this grace in which we stand, and we rejoice in our sufferings, knowing that our suffering produces endurance, and endurance produces character, and character produces hope, and hope does not put us to shame, because God's love has been poured into our hearts through the Holy Spirit who has been given to us. For while we were still weak, at the right time Christ died for the ungodly."

Sara nurtures her relationship with Jesus in a multitude of different ways. She commented, "Boiled down, it's scripture intake, prayer, and Bible memory." She attends church regularly with her husband and daughter, having sweet fellowship with the congregation afterwards. During the week, her goal is to start her day with thirty minutes of Scripture reading, praying before for her heart and afterwards for the response to what she has read. Sara shares, "Admittedly, on the days I wake up super early for work, I don't usually sit and read. However, I listen to a sermon while I am getting ready for work." She uses a large chunk of her driving commute time to and from work to pray for a variety of things in her life. Some examples of this are praying for herself, family, friends, co-workers, high schoolers at her church, and unbelievers. Sara shares, "I keep this all straight using the PrayerMate app." Some of the time, she will use some of the drive time to and from work to just worship through music. When Sara is having a hard time praying because of her attitude, she finds that worship sets her heart right. Throughout her day, during little pockets of time, she uses the Fighter Verses app to work on reviewing memorized scripture. Sara shared, "I think an important part in all of this is thankfulness." Sara definitely has a heart posture of an attitude of gratitude most of the time. She thanks God for the people and circumstances that she is praying for, and thanks Him for the things He has given her or done already. Sara shared, "Not just going into prayer bearing my heart and making demands, but reminding myself of the truth." Which is why Sara thinks that Bible memory is extremely important. She goes on to explain, "It keeps us grounded in truth when the world around us seems to be falling apart, and helps our prayers to be in line with God's will."

The talents and gifts that God has blessed Sara with are in the area of music, being a mom, being a people person, being a good communicator, and being an open book to others. Sara commented, "Like every person and every gift, I have twisted what God has given." All gifts can be used for good or evil. She explained that by no means has she used these gifts perfectly or completely selflessly. However, through singing, God has opened doors for her to help lead worship music. Sara added, "The combination of a passion for motherhood and a long wait while He has refined me, has caused me to take my role as a mother very seriously, and I am intentional about what I do and why I do it, regarding parenting and building that relationship." Sara's personality and communication skills have been helpful in teaching high school girls at her church and opening up Gospel conversations with co-workers and family members. Sara closes with, "Being an open book has helped me be very vulnerable, honest, and transparent with people about my wrestlings and victories through Jesus."

James 1:2-4

"Consider it pure joy, my brothers and sisters, whenever you face trials of many kinds, because you know that the testing of your faith produces perseverance. Let perseverance finish its work so that you may be mature and complete, not lacking anything."

CHAPTER 12

FAITH & LOSS & DEVASTATION

Annie Maendel

Annie Maendel is an incredibly courageous and resilient woman of God. She has done so much for so many people in her life, and continues to leave a priceless legacy alongside her husband (Sam Maendel), who passed away on December 8th of 2021. She comes from a Hutterite background and excels in various areas such as cooking, cleaning, knitting, and raising a family of eight children; no small task. Annie has also offered her services to all her daughters-in-law, including me, to help them during their deliveries of their babies. Annie was so special to me personally during the time our son, Joshua, was born. Josh was born via an emergency C-section with the cord wrapped tightly around his neck. There was an additional hospital stay that was needed before he could come home with us. Annie stayed at the hospital with me and taught me everything I needed to know about being a first-time mother. When we were able to bring Josh home with us, she stayed on and cooked meals and cleaned our home while I was recovering from my C-section. Annie opted for an in-person interview with me. I had forwarded my "Jesus Questions" to her beforehand, so she was well prepared to share her responses with me. I have listened to our session together multiple times, taken notes, and hope and pray that I can bring justice to her beautiful story about loss and the legacy she and her husband leave behind.

Annie commented, "God has given us the grace to fulfill our desire to be missionaries and take care of other people. We were able to go to Guatemala and minister to women and children there." Sam and Annie were able to serve the people in Guatemala for about five years until Sam got very sick. They had to pull away from that missionary work and tend to Sam in the United States, as he underwent his lung transplant surgery. Annie shares, "I am so glad I got the chance to do that with Sam while he was still alive and raise our family of eight children together." Both Sam and Annie did an incredible job of raising a household of eight children. They worked together, sharing various chores of the household and tending to each of their children to make their home run smoothly and efficiently. Sam drove a semi-truck, and Annie owned and operated her own daycare at home, so Annie did the majority of childcare on a daily basis. Sam liked to plan vacations for the family and individual dates to spend with his children when he was off the road from his trucking career. Sam spent an enormous amount of time praying over his bride and children while he was driving across the country in his truck. Annie commented, "I did feel alone for a majority of that time up until I started to travel with him after our family was raised and out of the home."

She continued to share through tears, "Dad died before me, and when Dad died... I miss him so much. I am so afraid of what could happen to me now." Annie had a minor stroke called a transient ischemic attack (TIA) the morning of the day she did this interview with me. Her daughter, Louisa, described that she could not use her legs or speak coherently for a brief period of time. The emergency EMTs were called, and all her vitals were normal, so she did not go into the hospital to be checked out. Annie shared, "I just trust the Lord that He will take care of me and bring me through. He's always there for me." God gave Annie the strength and courage to move forward in life after she lost Sam. Annie shared, "I was able to get better with the Lord's help. I was able to walk the walk with Him."

Annie was about ten years old when the Lord spoke to her as she was walking to the kitchen for some jam for her toast, "He showed me, through my love for Maya people or Indians and desire to serve others, that I was going to help women and children someday in that capacity." Annie was very excited to know that she would be able to accomplish something like this in life, and she wanted to be part of helping this specific population of women and children. She shared, "God made it very clear to me that I was supposed to be part of all this." Annie and Sam got the opportunity to go to Guatemala multiple times over the course of five years to teach this population a multitude of different things. They helped educate them about caring for their children, and helped others receive wheelchairs when they had physical limitations and abilities. They developed some very close bonds of friendship with the people in Guatemala, and she and Sam learned a great deal from them, too. This was the opportunity that the Lord had spoken to Annie about early on in her life, and she and her husband lived it out.

Their ministry in Guatemala came to an abrupt halt due to Sam's health condition. Annie shared, "We came back to the states; however, his health did not get any better." Sam was on oxygen for a while prior to needing a lung transplant. He got the lung transplant surgery done and seemed to be doing better. Annie shared, "I remember during the time of recovery, after the lung transplant surgery, that we almost lost him. Sam was declared clinically dead for forty minutes, and our family prayed over him. That time, he walked out of the hospital alive. It was a true miracle!" Sam and Annie continued to lead a low-key life together, with him driving the school bus routes each day to help provide for them. Annie shared, "Over time, he lost most of his appetite and would not eat the meals I had prepared for him." Sam had a few minor strokes prior to going into the hospital on December 7th, 2021. He had fallen down and scraped his face, and they brought him into the hospital to clean up his wounds on his face. He never made it out of the hospital alive. Annie shared, "I thought I was just taking my husband in to help clean up his face, and I was preparing our home for his return. It absolutely crushed me that he did not return. Annie shared, "He died in the hospital on December 8, 2021. This was the most painful thing I have ever gone through in my life. It also has been very painful moving forward in life and trying to cope without him today. The Lord continues to give me strength and courage even though I lost my love and everything I wanted to do and be. The Lord gives me grace through this; I have been really struggling with this for a while." Annie is frightened now when stuff happens, and she does not know what to think of it, like the minor stroke that happened to her yesterday. Annie shares, "I just pray. I hold up everything to Him and lean on Jesus!"

Annie shares her relationship with Jesus today, "I love my Lord. He is everything to me. He is what I need! I know I have a family that loves and supports me, and I just have to give it all up to Jesus." Annie listens to Scripture readings from the Bible. It is more difficult for her to read these days, so she listens to the Bible on tape and her Christian television programs that help nurture her relationship with Jesus Christ. Annie shares, "It is difficult to be alone when others in the household need to go to different places during the day. I know Louisa is going to leave her job and come stay with me all the time, and this brings me comfort. My family has been better about remembering to call and communicate with me as well on a regular basis. The Lord will continue to be my Rock, and I will rely solely on Him."

Special Tribute to Sam Maendel:

"Thank you, Sam and Annie Maendel, for all you have taught and done for our entire family, and the beautiful legacy you have left over all these years."

Romans 8:38-39

"For I am convinced that neither death nor life, neither angels nor demons, neither the present nor the future, nor any powers, neither height nor depth, nor anything else in all creation, will be able to separate us from the love of God that is in Christ Jesus our Lord."

Christine Young

Christine Young is an amazing child of God and has a miraculous story of faith, determination, grit, and valor. She has been my best friend since ninth grade in high school, and we are very close to this day. She opted for a phone interview and gave me permission to record our session together. I had forwarded my "Jesus Questions" to her beforehand, so she was well prepared to share her responses with me. This story hits close to home, and as you read it, you will understand why. I hope and pray that I am able to retell this incredible story of faith and God's love, mercy, grace, and forgiveness to honor everyone in her story.

Jesus has most impacted Christine's life through guiding her on a path that she never thought she could achieve. He has shown her things she never thought she would be capable of. He was there for her when she was down and helped her get through some very dark times in life. The most painful incident that Christine has been through was a devastating car accident she was involved in with her little brother, Shore, and his fianceé, Kara.

On July 5th, 1992, she was in a severe car accident North of Elkader, Iowa. Her brother and his fianceé died in the accident. She was taken to Elkader Hospital, and from there she was air evacuated to Iowa City. Christine was told that she spent two to three months in a coma in Iowa City. After Iowa City, they moved her to Covenant Hospital in

Waterloo, Iowa. Her mother, Cindy, was there for her through everything, and she was her rock during this entire situation. Christine's dad, Russ, was also a huge encouragement to her. Cindy would mark on the calendar, as Christine would have various visitors that summer. Christine's mother lived with Ann Ellsworth and Carmen Maendel (Phelps) that summer in Iowa City, and Cindy and Carmen visited Christine every day at the hospital together that summer. When Christine got back to Covenant Hospital in Waterloo, IA, her mom and dad told her that her brother had died in the accident. They told her that Shore was in Heaven coaching God's little league baseball team, and that was what he was called to do. Christine shared with me, "I felt like I was left behind, but I knew God had a purpose for me and I did not know what at the time." After she got out of the hospital, she went to Goodwill Industries for rehabilitation, and then she lived on her own again, just like she had prior to the accident. She resumed her work position she was in before the car accident. Since then, she has met a lot of people, and one who stuck out to her was Linda Walton. She was a very Godly woman and an incredible mentor for Christine at that time. Christine feels that God miraculously allowed her to live so that she could help others who were going through rough times. She helped out a co-worker when he was struggling. This co-worker of Christine's kept asking her why she was helping him. She shared with me, "I was doing it because I cared, and God told me that he needed help." He is not a believer in Jesus Christ. Christine told me that she tried to give this back to God; however, she felt He was still encouraging her to help out this man at her workplace. She continues to minister to both women and men out at her workplace today.

Christine shared the details of the accident with me next, and it is truly a miracle that she is alive today. Two through six ribs, her right clavicle, and all the bones in her face were completely broken or shattered. She had to learn how to walk, talk, eat, etc., all over again. Both her mom and dad were there for her and extremely supportive of Christine at this time. Christine shared with me, "I believe God allowed me to live so that I could share with others about Him and all the amazing things He has done in my life for me, especially with this car accident." She feels that God wants her to inspire people to return to church and toward a personal relationship with Jesus Christ. She has helped out so many people. Christine feels tremendously blessed to be here today, and she does not know how she could have done it without God by her side. She does not remember anything except that she put her foot on the gas right before the accident happened. This was the last thing she remembered. They were in a truck and hit another vehicle head-on. It is undetermined if she fell asleep and crossed the center line or if the other truck did. The accident report did implicate Christine as at fault in this accident; however, if she did fall asleep at the wheel, then the oncoming car may have swerved to get out of her way. There was no evidence of this. Christine stated, "I have never in my life before falling asleep at the wheel, and have always been careful in that area." Christine's mom thinks that God will let her remember when He feels she is ready. Christine stated, "I must not be ready yet."

One small side note here: I told you this story was very close to my heart. I spent quite a bit of time with Christine and her family growing up; I was close with her entire family. Christine had invited me to go to the river with them over the 4th of July weekend of 1992. I was planning on going with them and decided, for some reason, at the last minute, to back out. I remember the dreaded phone call I received about this accident on the morning of July 5th. For many years, I felt that if only I were there, I could have somehow helped prevent this devastating accident from happening. Recently, within the last year, I asked Christine for forgiveness for not being there, and she assured me that there is no forgiveness to seek in this situation. Christine and I went to visit Shore's grave and spoke to him for about five hours straight on my last visit back to Waterloo, Iowa, the summer of 2024. We both had the opportunity to share our hearts openly with him that day, and believe we found some sort of closure and path for God to heal our hearts.

Jesus showed up through nurses and doctors, because there were several doctors who predicted that Christine would not make it. One day in particular, Cindy and Carmen walked around in a complete daze when they were told that Christine was not going to make it. There was one doctor who told her mom that she would make it out of there alive. That doctor had faith in Christine, and Christine has a very strong faith in Jesus Christ as well. She wants everything to happen, not in her time, but in God's time. She shared with me, "I believe that things happen for a reason, and the only one that knows that reason is God himself." Christine believes that God wanted her to walk through this experience to help humble her a bit when she needed a little more humility in her life. God has inspired Christine through returning to church and has encouraged others to join her as well. She has inspired her friend, Jackie, to come to church with her several times now. She is trying to do the work that God wants her to do, fulfilling her purpose in life.

Christine stated, "If God did not allow the car accident to happen, then I would not know where I would be today spiritually." Today, she learns to live each day with joy and appreciation to be alive. She dances in the hallway on her breaks at work, and sometimes encourages others to join in as well. She says she has taken work too seriously for too long. She feels that as long as she is fulfilling the requirements of her job, no one should have a problem with that. Sometimes, managers and supervisors even dance with her. She loves to dance in the middle of the day to Godly music. She shows her gratitude through dance, and she is thankful for everything God has done for her and has provided for her in her life. She shared with me, "That accident made my life turn around." She has learned that you don't judge people, and you need to learn to accept them for who they are. She warns others about "judging a book by its cover" or making judgments about someone that they don't even know. She feels that she owes it all to God. Christine commented, "If God was not there for me in my darkest times, I never would have been pulled out of my pit of despair." She praises Jesus every day and thanks God that she has been woken up each morning. She prays for people that she doesn't even know, and when she walks the parking lot on her lunch break, she has her hands in the air and is praying to God. She thanks God for everything she has ever gotten from Him. She will continue to try to lift others up with discernment and encouragement, and help other people feel loved by Jesus. She encourages others to seek God and have Him help them in various areas of their lives. Christine feels that it is important to get out of her comfort zone and do things that are maybe challenging and not convenient. She continues to listen to God and pay attention to how he directs her steps to help others in her life path. She continually plants seeds in others and allows God to do the rest. Christine's story emphasizes that even when unexpected events occur, God can still work for our good and has a plan in place.

Romans 8:28

"And we know that in all things God works for the good of those who love him, who have been called according to his purpose."

Emma Braaten

Emma Braaten is a very courageous and blessed young woman. She has a powerful testimony story of where she came from and who she is today, all because of Jesus! She has found her true identity in Christ and loves to share her story with others, as encouragement to them, on their own life journey. Emma opted to email her responses to my "Jesus Questions" to me, and she gave me permission to share her story in this book, using the responses she emailed back to me.

Emma shared, "Jesus saved me from the death of addiction. He changed me and molded me into the woman of God I was proposed to be." He not only saved her and changed her, but He gifted Emma with an opportunity for a better, more fulfilling life; a life filled with purpose in Him.

Emma goes on to explain, "When I was eight years old, I was sexually abused by my dad; that continued for two consecutive years." She kept it a secret from everyone until she was twenty-one years old. Emma shared, "It took me thirteen years to see Jesus in the sexual abuse. Jesus took that horrible thing that happened to me, and He showed me forgiveness." Jesus showed Emma that she can shine His light in others' lives who have been through similar things. She shared, "He helped me forgive my dad." She wrote her dad a letter telling him all the things she resented him for, and all the things she had held against him. Emma commented, "Jesus showed me how to forgive him. Jesus helped me write a letter telling my dad that, although I didn't excuse the things he had done to me, that I forgave him, and I left the rest between him and God." A huge physical weight lifted off of her the day she mailed that letter. The Holy Spirit filled that hurtful place in her heart and mind. Emma shared, "God has given me many opportunities to help others who have been in a similar situation, and I have been able to encourage them in the Lord."

Emma continued sharing her story, "My story starts when I was eight years old, and I was sexually abused by my dad." When she was ten years old, her dad became very sick. He had a rare disease that only thirteen other people in the world had, and it was called "recurrent kidney stones." He would pass anywhere between two hundred and fifty and three hundred kidney stones at one time. This disease caused a lot of other health issues for him. He was unable to work after some time due to the constant pain. Emma's mom started going to school to become a nurse at this time, and she worked overnight at a nursing home to provide for her family. Emma shared, "My dad was incredibly manipulative. He was the type of person who could leave any conversation, making you feel as if it was all your fault." Just to paint a picture for you, one time she wrote down everything she wanted to tell him and talk to him about, so that she didn't lose track of her thoughts and feelings in the conversation. Emma commented, "I still left that conversation feeling as if all of my thoughts and emotions were wrong, even though I had physically written down what I genuinely felt at that time." Her dad was sick; as a ten-year-old, you don't realize you have the option to take responsibility for your sick parent or stay a kid a little longer. Emma shared, "I grew up quite a bit faster due to the difficult circumstances."

They didn't have a lot of money, and life was stressful. She tried coping with her depression and anger the right way for a few years. She was in lots of plays and musicals. Emma shared, "I have been in forty-three productions ranging from plays to musicals to competitive acting (one-act plays)." She was on the speech and tennis team for seven tennis teams for seven years, and the varsity captain for two years. She played basketball and softball competitively. She played drums for the band, the jazz band, and the pep band. She was in choir, a cappella choir, and show choir, performing solos and ensembles regularly. Emma shared, "Everything I did, I tried to become anyone but who I really was. Eventually, none of those things were enough to mask the pain and depression I had."

Emma commented, "When I was sixteen years old, that was the first time I did drugs." She started with weed (marijuana) and progressed to pills. She shared, "I was finally good at something, getting high and selling drugs." When she was a junior in high school, her parents legally separated. She dove deeper into her addiction with each passing year. Emma explained, "My senior year of high school was where my addiction took me to a whole new level; a person I genuinely didn't know." She was constantly high, and it was the first time she tried meth. She fell in love with it. Emma shared, "Getting high did for me what nothing else could; it masked the pain and helped me 'get away' from the problems in my life, or so I thought." She ended up getting in some trouble in her senior year; however, she was a good student all the years leading up to that. She graduated from high school with honors and went to college in Fergus Falls, MN.

Emma's addiction worsened when she moved into her own apartment. Emma shared, "My newfound freedom gave me opportunities to use and sell drugs in a way I hadn't had before." She wound up in a toxic relationship with someone who was also using meth. Emma commented, "Within six months of using meth, almost daily, I lost both of my jobs, dropped out of college, my car broke down, and I lost my apartment." It took everything from me, including the last shred of who I was before drugs. Meth changed everything about her. It robbed her joy, her kindness, everything she once was; she was the opposite on meth. She explained, "I had nothing and turned to drugs to solve my problems." Emma ended up doing a string of burglaries to pay for her addiction. She got arrested for possession of stolen property and went to jail for a few days. She got bailed out and went on the run from everything and everyone. Emma shared, "I disappeared from my family; they had no clue where I was or if I was even alive." She had run away to California. She turned again to the only thing she knew: drugs and crime. Emma commented, "I found myself deeper in my addiction than I had ever been before." After eight months, Emma was stranded in Las Vegas with nothing but the clothes on her back. She reached out to her mom for the first time in eight months. Her mom told her, "I will help you come home if you turn yourself in for the burglaries when you arrive here." Emma agreed to turn herself in. Emma shared, "I came home, and when I stepped off that bus, my mom, my uncle, and my grandpa were all standing there with open arms waiting to hug me." She couldn't believe the love they were willing to show her after everything she put them through.

Emma continued to explain, "I spent five and a half months in jail and acquired four felonies. I wish I could say that was rock bottom for me, but it wasn't." After she got out of jail, she relapsed on meth a month later and continued her path of devastating destruction. She shared, "I ended up absconding from probation and going back to California." She told no one where she was going, leaving her family hoping she was alive somewhere once again. Emma shared, "I couldn't go back to the people I had met the year prior in California because I had burned those bridges." She found herself, once again, even deeper in her addiction than she had known before. Emma commented, "I turned to meth and crime, again." She had always told herself that she would never use a needle to get high, and if she ever did, it would be her last time.

Emma shared even deeper, "About five months after absconding, I allowed someone to get me high using a needle. They overdosed me and left me lying on the floor for three days, alone. When I woke up three days later, I was in the same spot on the floor alone; no one else was in the house with me." Emma ended up reaching out to a good friend of hers from college. Emma called her and talked to her. Her friend asked Emma what she was doing and why she wouldn't come home. Emma shared painfully, "I had a very real thought at the time that I would rather die at the age of twenty than spend five years in prison." She eventually came to some version of normality and came home to Minnesota.

When she got to Minnesota, she was immediately arrested and spent six months in jail. Emma shared, "Jesus reached me that time." She was sitting in a Bible study when one of the volunteers looked at her and said, "Emma, you're going to go to MN Adult and Teen Challenge, and you are going to become the woman God proposed you to be." That was the first time the Lord spoke through someone else to reach her. Emma commented, "I did end up going to MN Adult and Teen Challenge when I was released from jail." Emma's heart was filthy and filled with bitterness, unforgiveness, resentment, and so much more. She had finally come to a place where God sat her down and said, "Emma, give me everything". That really meant *everything*. Emma shared, "Every form of a person I had tried to be over the years, every thought, every emotion, or lack thereof, every mask I wore; God wanted to take it all." Through the yearlong program at MN Adult and Teen Challenge, God transformed her. He transformed her heart and her mind. Emma spoke cheerfully, "I was changed from the inside out." She spent time in the Word of God, healing her heart and mind.

While she was in the program, her mom was given the opportunity to work there as a nurse, and she has worked there to this day. Emma beamed, "There were so many God moments that happened, too many to count." After she graduated from the yearlong program, she entered into another yearlong program that they offered, which was called the Teen Challenge Leadership Institute. It's a yearlong transitional living program that includes biblical classes, basic life skills classes, etc. While she was there, she started interning for the Long-Term Women's program. After her time at the leadership institute was done, she was given a job there to work with the clients. She had a lot of jobs while she worked there for six full years. She worked in Long-Term Women's, Short-Term Women's, and Admissions with this program. Emma shared, "The first year I was working there, the Lord asked me if I wanted my oldest brother back in our lives from his addiction." He was struggling with a meth addiction as well. She prayed for him every day for a year. Almost exactly a year later, he entered the Rochester site of MN Adult and Teen Challenge. Emma shared, "God moved so mightily in his life!" He restored and redeemed so many aspects of Emma's life as well.

She met her husband through the Leadership program. They became friends and led worship together quite often. About a year and a half later, they started dating. They dated for only a short couple of months before Emma broke up with him. She shared, "I wasn't emotionally ready to be in a relationship; I didn't know it at that time, but it was mine to own up to, too." A year and a half passed, and during that time, God healed her emotions in a major way. The Lord started bringing Dan back into her life again. Emma commented, "At that time, I apologized to him for my actions and asked him for another chance." A few months later, they were engaged and ready to start their life together. She shared, "It has been the most beautiful gift to be married to him." They have two beautiful sons, and they get to serve the Lord alongside one another. They have seen God move in and through their lives in so many ways. Emma concluded, "To sum up my story of how God got a hold of me: when I finally chose to let go of the nothing that I had, I encountered the Holy Spirit, I was loved by the Father, and I found my life in Jesus. His thoughts are higher than our thoughts, His thoughts are not our thoughts, and His ways are not our ways. His word does not return void; it will accomplish what He pleases, and it shall prosper in the thing in which He has sent it.

Emma's relationship with Jesus today is the thing she cherishes most. She shared, "He is my friend, my savior, my everything. I spend time in prayer, in His Word, in worship, and with the body of Christ. My husband and I have our marriage built on the foundation of Jesus Christ." They serve their sons and lead them in their salvation, in Jesus. Her husband is the Youth Pastor at their church. They serve the youth alongside one another, and she helps lead worship there about once a month. There are many aspects of their life where they open their home up to those in need of ministry, guidance, love, and friendship.

Emma summarizes her devotion to our Lord, "I spend time in the Word, I do devotionals with friends, I worship Him through song, I spend time in prayer, and I do my best to make room to listen to Him as well. I allow myself to be open and led by the Holy Spirit. I cherish the gift of life and all of the things that come along with it." Emma has always been interested in singing throughout her entire life. She comments on one time in particular, "I remember after I was filled with the Holy Spirit when I was in the MN Adult and Teen Challenge Program, I sang one Sunday in the choir and this voice I had never heard came singing through me. It was a gift that God gave me to share with others. Since then, I have been singing His praises." She has been given the gift of prayer, the gift of exhortation, and the gift of healing many times since being filled with the Spirit.

Emma concludes with this,

"I have been leading worship and singing since I was filled with the Spirit in 2012. I lead worship at our church, in our home, at other churches, at women's events, and others. It's amazing to be leading worship and watching chains fall off of people, to watch people become free in Jesus through music. It's as much a gift to me as it is to share it. I pray for others as often as I can. I am in the process of writing a prayer book. I send texts to others with prayers, I call them and pray for them, and I pray with them the moment they ask for prayer. I do my best to lift others and encourage them not only in their gifting and their talents, but also in those moments of hardship. Praying for healing for others is amazing to witness God move in that. I have had the privilege of watching people be healed through prayer. It's a beautiful moment, and seeing God show up changes people's faith in a single moment."

1 Peter 5:8-9

"Be sober-minded; be watchful. Your adversary the devil prowls around like a roaring lion, seeking someone to devour. Resist him, firm in your faith, knowing that the same kinds of suffering are being experienced by your brotherhood throughout the world."

Marlyn I. Duus

Marlyn is a bold and courageous woman who is on fire for God. She allows the adversity in her life to help make her stronger and more resilient, instead of breaking her down. Our extended families have known each other for multiple decades now, and Marlyn is a true gem and friend for life. I hope I am able to do justice to her beautiful, heartfelt testimony and love for our Lord, Jesus Christ. She opted to have me email her my "Jesus Questions" and brought her answers personally to my front door. Marlyn has given me permission to share her story in this book, using the responses she gave to me.

Jesus Christ has always been Marlyn's best friend for most of her life since the second grade. After watching *Billy Graham Crusades* on their new television, she repented and gave her heart to God. After that prayer, she had such a thirst to learn more about Him in Sunday School. Marlyn's father passed away when she was in the eighth grade, and a relative was undergoing an eating disorder. Marlyn commented, "Despite these trials, God was walking beside me." God eventually guided her to her husband, Mark, who also loves the Lord. They will be celebrating their 46th wedding anniversary this coming April.

The most painful incident that they went through, as a couple, was the short life of their second daughter, Jessica Hannah. Marlyn recalls, "She had been so 'active' in my womb. We watched Jessica on her first stage performance of her ultrasound, as she did a front double flip somersault and then disappeared on the screen." Jessica was born with a rare birth defect, so they read up on this with as much information as they could to try to help Jessica face the battle of that defect. At four and a half months old, Jessica was hospitalized and eventually died of sepsis.

Marlyn shared, "We will be reunited with her in Heaven someday." They still had one healthy daughter, Joy, and did not have peace that she would be their only child. Mark and Marlyn applied for adoption through their county and were refused since they already had a child of their own. After four miscarriages and many tears, they were blessed with their third daughter, Melody.

Jesus showed up and encouraged this couple through various Scriptures in the Bible. Psalms 91:3-4, "Surely He shall deliver you from the snare of the fowler and from the perilous pestilence. He shall cover you with His feathers, and under His wings you shall take refuge." Marlyn shared, "The Lord gave me these two verses in my morning devotions before Jessica was taken to the Children's Hospital. These verses gave me comfort as we were facing decisions for our daughter, Jessica."

Marlyn rejoiced in stating, "Four years later, the Lord covered me with His peace as I faced an actual pregnancy that I could carry full term. Certain relatives would panic against this pregnancy, but I clung to God's peace!" The end result was a beautiful, healthy daughter, whom they named Melody. At this time, Marlyn told the Lord that their family was complete; however, other family members did not agree because Joy wanted a brother. Marlyn recalls, "My parents (Emil and Victoria) always taught me to respect human life—even preborn babies. 'It's Life,' they would say, no matter what circumstances the baby would be conceived under." Her dad, Emil Duda, had died twenty years before then; however, Marlyn had a memory of him reviving a kitten that she had accidentally run over with her bike. At that very moment, Marilyn declared, "That memory was brought back to me as I struggled with this next unplanned pregnancy. 'It's Life' were the words I heard inside my head." This kept going over in her mind, and Jacob Mark was born eight months later.

Today, Marlyn has a healthy and vibrant relationship with the utmost reverence for our Lord. She commented, "My relationship with Jesus keeps growing. Sometimes, there are stagnant times, but God is so gracious, loving, and forgiving. Even during those times, there is so much to learn from Him." Marlyn has devotional reading in the Bible every morning. She commented, "Daily reading of the Psalms and Proverbs is the first thing I do in the morning." Marlyn reads four chapters in the Bible daily so that she can complete reading through the entire Bible every year. She shared, "This is also my time to intercede in prayer for my family, our nation, and other prayer requests. After this quiet time with the Lord, it helps me seek God's purpose for the day since each day is a gift from Him."

God has blessed Marlyn with God fearing parents and older siblings to learn to develop patience and be a living example of God's grace. Marlyn shared, "When people see me, I pray that they can see Jesus." She is living this out on a daily basis in her workplace. She works with Middle School Special Needs students, which gives her a strong purpose for her life. Marlyn is also a voice for the unborn and has been teaching parenting classes for a number of years now. Marlyn commented, "This has been my special calling for the last several years."

Psalms 127:3-4

"Children are a heritage from the Lord, offspring a reward from Him. Like arrows in the hands of a warrior are children born in one's youth."

Inspirational Stories, Bible Verses & Prayers

(These are some Inspirational and Motivational Stories I used to train my Maendel Fitness "Fitness & Nutrition" clients in our gym for eight years; they are also included in my online program I created in 2022, Rock Hard Body "Power, Strength & Fitness".)

"A Wise Man's Jokes"
(Author Unknown)

A wise man once faced a group of people who were complaining about the same issue over and over again. One day, out of the blue, he told them a joke instead of listening to all of them complaining, and everyone cracked up laughing.

Then, the man repeated the joke. He got a few smiles.

Finally, the man repeated the joke the third time, **but no one reacted.**

The man smiled and said, "You won't laugh at the same joke more than once, so what are you getting out of continuing to complain about the same problem?"

Moral:

You are not going to make headway if you keep complaining about the same problem, but do nothing to try to fix it. Don't waste your time complaining while expecting others to react to your complaints. Instead, take action to make a positive change. You should not worry about your problems because by worrying, you will not be able to solve them; instead, you will waste your time and energy.

Philippians 4:6-7

"Do not be anxious about anything, but in every situation,
by prayer and petition, with

thanksgiving, present your requests to God. And the peace of God,
which transcends all understanding, will guard your hearts and your
minds in Christ Jesus."

PRAYER

Heavenly Father,

Help me, Lord, to trust You completely with every concern. May I not be consumed by anxiety or fear, but instead find peace in Your presence and in Your promises.

I thank You, Father, for Your faithfulness throughout this day. In every moment, You have been my strength and my refuge. I offer You my gratitude for Your constant provision and care.

Grant me the courage to bring all my needs and desires before You in prayer. May my petitions be aligned with Your will, knowing that You hear and answer according to Your perfect plan.

Father, I surrender my heart to Your peace, which surpasses all understanding. Guard my thoughts and emotions with Your peace.

All these things I pray in the precious Holy name of Jesus Christ, AMEN.

"Breathing with No Air"
(Author Unknown)

A boy once asked a wise old man what the secret to success is. After listening to the boy's question, the wise man told the boy to meet him at the river in the morning, and he would be given the answer there.

In the morning, the wise man and the boy began walking toward the river. They continued on into the river, past the point where the water covered their nose and mouth. At this time, the wise man ducked the boy into the water.

As he struggled to get out, the wise man continued to push him further down. The boy felt a fish slip by his leg and squirmed to get up even harder. The man eventually pulled the boy's head up so he could get air. The boy gasped as he inhaled a deep breath of air.

The wise man said, 'What were you fighting for when you were underwater?" The boy replied, "Air!" The man said, **"There you have the secret to success."** When you want to gain success as much as you wanted air when you were underwater, you will obtain it. That's the only secret."

Moral:

Success starts with the desire to achieve something. If your motivation is weak, your results will follow suit. Think about what you desire the most in life and work towards getting it. Don't allow your environment or other people to influence the things that you truly want. Just because the fish swimming by is comfortable with being underwater doesn't mean that you are. The story highlights the idea that even when we feel like we are at the end of our rope, our breath is not solely dependent on physical air, but can be a conduit to a deeper spiritual connection, a reminder of Jesus, who sustains us through even the harshest of circumstances.

Psalms 1:1-3

"But whose delight is in the law of the LORD, and who meditates on his law day and night. That person is like a tree planted by streams of water, which yields its fruit in season and whose leaf does not wither—whatever they do prospers."

PRAYER

Dear Heavenly Father,

Lord, help me be like a tree planted by streams of water, which yields its fruit in season and whose leaf does not wither. May I delight in the law of the Lord, meditating on it day and night. And because of your word planted deep, may whatever I do prosper and bring glory to Your name. All these things I pray in the precious Holy name of Jesus Christ, AMEN.

"Cherish Your Struggles"
"Author Unknown"

One day, a girl came upon a cocoon, and she could tell that a butterfly was trying to hatch. She waited and watched the butterfly struggle for hours to release itself from the tiny hole. All of a sudden, the butterfly stopped moving—it seemed to be stuck.

The girl then decided to help get the butterfly out. She went home to get a pair of scissors to cut open the cocoon. The butterfly was then easily able to escape; however, its body was swollen, and its wings were underdeveloped.

The girl still thought she had done the butterfly a favor as she sat there waiting for its wings to grow in order to support its body. However, that wasn't happening. The butterfly was unable to fly, and for the rest of its life, it could only move by crawling around with little wings and a large body.

Despite the girl's good intentions, she didn't understand that **the restriction of the butterfly's cocoon and the struggle the butterfly had to go through in order to escape served an important purpose.** As butterflies emerge from tight cocoons, it forces fluid from their body into their wings to prepare them to be able to fly.

Moral:

The struggles that you face in life help you grow and get stronger. There is often a reason behind the requirement of doing hard work and being persistent. When enduring difficult times, you will develop the necessary strength that you'll need in the future. Without having any struggles, you won't grow, which means it's very important to take on personal challenges for yourself rather than relying on other people to always help you. Our struggles help us develop strengths, and without struggles, we do not grow or get any stronger in life.

Isaiah 40:31

"But those who hope in the Lord will renew their strength.
They will soar on wings like eagles; they will run and not grow weary,
they will walk and not be faint."

PRAYER

Heavenly Father,

I thank You for the promise of Isaiah 40:31. Help me wait on You and trust in Your unfailing love, so that I may renew my strength and soar like eagles. Give me the courage to run with endurance, walk with confidence, and overcome any challenges that I may face. All these things I pray in the precious Holy name of Jesus Christ, AMEN.

"Dirty Money"
(Author Unknown)

A well-respected speaker began a seminar by showing an audience of 150 people a crisp twenty-dollar bill. He asked, "Who wants this twenty-dollar bill?"

All 150 people nodded.

He said, "I am going to give this money to someone, but first..." Then, he proceeded to crumple the bill up.

He asked the crowd again if anyone wanted it.

All 150 hands went up in the air.

The speaker then dropped the money on the floor and stomped all over it.

He then raised it in the air to show the crowd. The money was filthy.

"Does anyone want it now?"

Every hand went up.

The speaker proceeded to tell the crowd that no matter what he did to ruin the money, people still wanted it because **its value remained the same.** It was still worth $20.

Life often beats us up to the point where we feel inadequate. We deal with bad circumstances and make bad choices that we have to deal with later. However, no matter what you go through, your value will remain the same. You have something special to offer that no one can take away from you.

Moral:

Life often beats us up to the point where we feel inadequate. We deal with bad circumstances and make bad choices that we have to deal with later. However, no matter what you go through, your value will remain the same. You have something special to offer that no one can take away from you.

Psalm 102:27

"But you remain the same, and your years will never end," which emphasizes that God, who is the source of our true worth, never changes and therefore our value in His eyes stays constant."

PRAYER

Heavenly Father,

You are mighty and strong, a solid rock, a safe hiding place. You are the stronghold of my life, the one who protects me from harm. Since You are my fortress, why am I afraid? Help me to know You so well, Lord, and to trust You so utterly, that fear has no place in my heart. All these things I pray in Jesus' precious Holy name, AMEN.

"Don't Hold Back"
(Author Unknown)

There was once a company whose CEO was very strict and often disciplined the workers for their mistakes or perceived lack of progress. One day, as the employees came into work, they saw a sign on the door that read, "Yesterday, the person who has been holding you back from succeeding in this company passed away. Please gather for a funeral service in the assembly room."

While the employees were saddened for the family of their CEO, they were also intrigued at the prospect of being able to now move up within the company and become more successful.

Upon entering the assembly room, many employees were surprised to see that the CEO was, in fact, present. They wondered among themselves, "If it wasn't he who was holding us back from being successful, who was it? Who has died?"

One by one, the employees approached the coffin, and upon looking inside, each was quite surprised. They didn't understand what they saw.

In the coffin, there was simply a mirror. So, when each employee looked in to find out who had been "holding them back from being successful," everyone saw themselves. Next to the mirror, there was a sign that read:

"The only person who is able to limit your growth is you. You are the only person who can influence your success. Your life changes when you break through your limiting beliefs and realize that you're in control of your life with God's guidance. The most influential relationship, aside from the one you have with Jesus Christ, is the relationship you have with yourself."

Moral:

The only person who is able to limit your growth is you. You are the only person who can influence your success. Your life changes when you break through your limiting beliefs and realize that you are in control of your life. The most influential relationship you can have, aside from your relationship with Jesus Christ, is the relationship you have with yourself. Now you know who has been holding you back from living up to your true potential. Are you going to keep allowing that person to hold you back?

Luke 4:18

"He came to proclaim freedom to prisoners and set the captives free. Jesus came to break off the limitations that are not from him and empower us to step into no limitations, full life, to accomplish everything God has called us to be and called us to do."

PRAYER

Heavenly Father,

I thank you, dear Father in heaven, for the many times you let me experience that I do not need to despair because of darkness, weakness, or sickness. You hear the desires of my heart. You love me for all that I love, when I love the Savior and when I praise His name. All these things I pray in Jesus' precious name, AMEN.

"Frogs for Dinner"
(Author Unknown)

A lady was once heating up a pot of water on a gas stove with the intent of cooking pasta for her family for dinner. A frog fell into the pot while it was sitting on the stove. While it wasn't his intention to be stuck in a pot of water, he didn't try to escape. He was comfortable enough as he was.

The lady soon turned on the flame to begin boiling the water. As the water's temperature began to rise, the frog was able to adjust his body temperature accordingly, so he remained in the pot without trying to do anything to change the situation.

However, as the water approached its boiling point, the frog's body temperature could no longer keep up. He finally tried to jump out of the pot, but with water temperature continuing to increase, he didn't have it in him to make the leap.

It was too late for the frog to save himself.

Moral:

Things don't always go as planned in life, and they certainly don't always go the way we want them to. But, no matter how bad a situation is, it's critical to be proactive and face the problem head-on. Unlike the frog, who waited until the last minute to try to do anything about the problem he was clearly facing, it's important to project the future outcomes of the obstacles that hinder you and mitigate them before they get past the point of no return. You have to avoid wasting time and take appropriate action before problems get out of hand or become too much to handle.

Colossians 3:23

"Work at everything you do with all your heart. Work as if you were working for the Lord, not for human masters."

PRAYER

Heavenly Father,

As I approach my daily tasks and responsibilities, I pray that I will work at everything with all my heart, as if I am working directly for You, not just for human approval; that in every action and word, I may strive to bring You glory and honor, doing all things with excellence and dedication, knowing that ultimately, it is You I am serving. In Jesus' precious name, AMEN.

"It's Never Too Late"
(Author Unknown)

In the 1940s, there was a man who, at the age of 65, was living off of $99 social security checks in a small house, driving a beat-up car.

He decided it was time to make a change, so he thought about what he had to offer that other people may benefit from. His mind went to his fried chicken recipe, which his friends and family loved.

He left his home state of Kentucky and traveled throughout the country, trying to sell his recipe to restaurants. He even offered the recipe for free, asking for only a small chunk of the money that was earned.

However, most of the restaurants declined his offer. In fact, 1,009 restaurants said no.

This story also demonstrates the power of persistence. You have to have confidence in yourself and believe in your work for other people to believe it, too. Disregard anyone who tells you "no" and simply move on.

But even after all of the rejections, he persisted. He believed in himself and his chicken recipe.

When he visited restaurant #1,010, he got a YES.

His name? Colonel Harland Sanders.

Moral:

There are a few lessons that you can take away from this story. First, it's never too late in life to find success. In a society that often celebrates young, successful people, it's easy to start to think you're never going to be successful after a certain age. However, Colonel Sanders is an example that proves that argument wrong, and perseverance in this particular example definitely pays off.

Hebrews 12:1-3

"Let us run with perseverance the race marked out for us, fixing our eyes on Jesus, the pioneer and perfecter of faith"

PRAYER

Heavenly Father,

I thank you for the example of Jesus, who endured the cross for my sake, and I ask that you help me fix my eyes on Him in the midst of my struggles and trials. Guide me to run the race set before me with perseverance, casting aside every weight and sin that hinders my progress. Strengthen me to not grow weary in doing good, knowing that the joy set before me is the prize of eternal life with you. In Jesus' name I pray, AMEN.

"It's Not That Complicated"
(Author Unknown)

There was once a very wise man living in ancient times. He was elderly and educated and held knowledge and books in the highest regard.

One day, while on a walk, he realized that his shoes were really starting to wear out. Because he spent a lot of time walking on a daily basis, he knew he had to find the best shoes to support and protect his feet. But, back then, this wasn't such an easy task, as he couldn't jump online to do some research and have shoes delivered to his door.

The man didn't want to make things worse by purchasing the wrong shoes and having inadequate protection, which would lead to injuries and the inability to leave his home and walk to find new books to read.

The man gathered all of the books he could that were written by only those whom he admired the most to search for the answer to his question, "What do I do if my shoes have fallen apart?"

He read through several books for many hours before finding out that he had no choice but to go buy a new pair of shoes. He then spent a lot of time reading about how to know if a pair of shoes fits properly. Once he was satisfied with the answers he found, he was proud of himself for doing the research, and he felt confident in his ability to buy a high-quality replacement for his old shoes. He figured if he hadn't done his research, he probably would have gone barefoot for the rest of his life, as he had no one to tell him how to fix his shoes.

Following the books' instructions, the man took a stick and measured his foot with it. He then went to the market and finally came upon a pair of shoes that he liked. However, he realized he had left the stick back at home, which was far away from the shop.

By the time the man returned to the market, the shop was closed. And, by that point, his shoes were completely split, so he had to return home barefoot.

The next morning, he walked back to the market with bare feet, but the shoes that he had chosen the day before had been sold. The wise man explained what had happened to the shopkeeper, who reacted with a sense of surprise, asking, **"Why didn't you buy the shoes yesterday?"**

The wise man replied, "Because I forgot the stick that I had used to measure my feet back home. And anyone who knows anything about shoes knows that you have to have the correct measurements of your feet before you can buy shoes. I didn't want to buy the wrong size, and I was following the normal instructions."

Even more confused, the shopkeeper asked, "But your foot was with you, why didn't you just try the shoes on?"

The wise man was equally confused in return and responded, "All the books say shoes must be bought with the exact same measurements of the shoes you already own."

Laughing, the shop owner replied, "Oh, no! You don't need the advice from books to buy shoes. You just need to have your feet, some money, and some common sense to not complicate things."

Moral:

Sometimes, you need to take action without overthinking things. Knowledge often comes in handy, but in some circumstances, if you lack experience or common sense, your knowledge will only get you so far. In fact, it could make things seem a lot more complicated than they actually are. If you're facing an issue, don't forget to use your reasoning skills in addition to anything you've learned in a formal learning environment.

Matthew 6:25-27

"Therefore I tell you, do not worry about your life, what you will eat or drink; or about your body, what you will wear. Is not life more than food, and the body more than clothes? Look at the birds of the air; they do not sow or reap or store away in barns, and yet your heavenly Father feeds them. Are you not much more valuable than they?"

PRAYER

Heavenly Father,

Thank you for reminding me that my life is more valuable than food and clothing, and that you, as my provider, will care for all my needs just as you care for the birds of the sky. When I feel anxious about tomorrow, help me to trust in your faithfulness and not let worry consume me. Grant me the peace that comes from knowing you are in control, and that you will provide everything I truly need today. In Jesus' precious name, AMEN.

"Jumping Frogs"
(Author Unknown)

A group of frogs was hopping through the forest when two of them accidentally hopped into a deep pit. The other frogs stood around the pit, and, seeing how deep it was, they told the two frogs that they couldn't help them—there was no hope.

However, fighting for their lives, the two frogs ignored the others and started to try jumping out of the pit.

The frogs at the top continued to tell the frogs in the pit to give up, as there was no way they would be able to jump out.

After trying over and over, one of the frogs listened to the others and gave up, accepting his fate and falling to his death. But the other frog continued to jump with all of his might. The crowd of frogs yelled down the pit for the frog to just stop—he wouldn't make it.

But the frog jumped even harder and persisted until he finally got out. Upon reaching the top, the other frogs said, "We thought there was no way any frog could jump that high; couldn't you hear us?"

The frog then signaled to the others that he was deaf, and **he thought that the frogs standing around the pit were encouraging him the whole time.**

Moral:

Some people's words can greatly impact your attitude and actions. Ignore the naysayers. Only engage with those who encourage you and believe in your ability to succeed. Furthermore, think about what you say to people before speaking, so you can make sure what you're saying is supportive. Your support (or lack thereof) could make the difference between success and failure for someone else.

Isaiah 41:10

*"Fear not, for I am with you; be not dismayed, for I am your God;
I will strengthen you, I will help you, I will uphold you with my
righteous right hand."*

PRAYER

Heavenly Father,

I am not afraid for I know that You are always with me to comfort me and to guide me. I will forever trust in You because I know that You will strengthen me in my times of despair. I find comfort knowing that You are God of all mankind and You will help me in my time of need. In Jesus' precious name, AMEN.

"Puppy Love"
(Author Unknown)

A pet shop owner got a new litter of puppies and was ready to sell them to their "forever" families. A young girl walked by the shop and noticed a sign saying, "Puppies for Sale," and of course was very eager to go inside.

She asked the owner, "How much do the puppies cost?" The owner replied, "They are all around $50."

The girl emptied her pocket change and told the store owner that she only had about $2, but she still wanted to look at them.

The shop owner whistled for the dogs, who came running down the hall of his shop. Five tiny fur balls, followed by one, limping behind the rest. The girl immediately singled out the lagging puppy and asked the store owner what was wrong with him.

The owner explained that the puppy was born with a deformity; he was missing a hip socket. This puppy would walk with a limp for the rest of its life.

The girl got excited, saying, "I want that puppy!"

The owner replied, "You don't want to buy that puppy. If you really want him, you can have him for free."

The girl got upset. She looked at the owner and said, "I don't want to have him for free. That puppy is worth just as much as the others. I'll give you the change I have now, and a dollar a month until I have paid for the puppy entirely."

The owner continued, "This dog is never going to be able to run and play like all of the other dogs. I think you're going to regret this decision."

To his surprise, **the girl reached down and rolled up her pant leg to reveal a crippled leg** that was supported by a large metal brace. She looked up at the owner and softly replied, 'Well, I'm not much of a runner, and this puppy needs someone who understands."

Moral:

Don't make assumptions about other people's wants, needs, or abilities. Every one of us has our own weaknesses, whether it's physical or mental. The trick is to not allow your weaknesses to slow you down and instead, find others in the world who can support you. Find and surround yourself with people who challenge you to reach your highest potential. The idea is to try to find strength in all your weaknesses and always rely on God's strength and not your own.

2 Corinthians 12:9

"My grace is sufficient for you,
for my power is made perfect in weakness."

PRAYER

Heavenly Father,

Thank you that Your grace meets me right where I am, especially in my weakest moments. I surrender my struggles and inadequacies to You, trusting that Your strength will shine through them. Help me lean into Your grace, knowing it's all I need to overcome any of my challenges. All these things I pray in the precious Holy name of Jesus Christ, AMEN.

"Rock Pebbles Sand"
(Stephen Covey)

A philosophy professor once stood up before his class with a large empty mayonnaise jar. He filled the jar to the top with large rocks and asked his students if the jar was full.

His students all agreed the jar was full.

He then added small pebbles to the jar and gave the jar a bit of a shake so that the pebbles could disperse themselves among the larger rocks. Then he asked again, **"Is the jar full now?"**

The students agreed that the jar was still full.

The professor then poured sand into the jar to fill up all the remaining empty space.

The students then agreed again that the jar was full.

The Metaphor:

In this story, the jar represents your life, and the rocks, pebbles, and sand are the things that fill up your life. The rocks represent the most important projects and things you have going on, such as spending time with your family and maintaining proper health. This means that if the pebbles and the sand were lost, the jar would still be full, and your life would still have meaning.

The pebbles represent the things in your life that matter, but that you could live without. The pebbles are certainly things that give your life meaning (such as your job, house, hobbies, and friendships), but they are not critical for you to have a meaningful life. These things often come and go, and are not permanent or essential to your overall well-being.

Finally, the sand represents the remaining filler things in your life, and material possessions. This could be small things such as watching television, browsing through your favorite social media site, or running errands. These things don't mean much to your life as a whole, and are likely only done to waste time or get small tasks accomplished.

Moral:

The metaphor here is that if you start by putting sand into the jar, you will not have room for rocks or pebbles. This holds true with the things you allow into your life. If you dedicate your time to the small and insignificant things, you will run out of room for the things that really matter in life. In order to have a more fulfilled life, pay attention to the "rocks" because they are critical to your long-term well-being.

Exodus 15:26

"If you will diligently listen to the voice of the LORD your God,
and will do that which is right in his eyes, and will pay attention to his
commandments, and keep all his statutes,
I will put none of the diseases on you, which I have put on the Egyptians;
for I am the LORD who heals you."

PRAYER

Heavenly Father,

As it says in Exodus 15:26, 'I am the Lord who heals you,' I come before you today humbly asking for Your healing touch in my life. Whether it be physical pain, emotional wounds, or spiritual struggles, I trust in Your power to restore me fully. Guide me to listen attentively to Your voice, to follow Your ways, and to obey Your commands, so that I may experience Your complete healing and wholeness. Thank you for Your love and faithfulness, in Jesus' precious name I pray, AMEN.

"Seeking Happiness"
(Author Unknown)

There were 200 people attending a seminar on mental and physical health. At one point, the speaker told the group they were going to do an activity. He gave each attendee one balloon and told them to write their name on it. Then, the balloons were collected and moved into a very small room.

The participants were then asked to go into the other room and were given two minutes to find their balloon.

It was chaos. People were searching frantically for their balloon, pushing each other and running into one another while they grabbed a balloon, looked at it, and inevitably tossed it to the side.

At the end of the two minutes, no one had found the balloon that had their name on it.

Then, the speaker asked the participants to go back into the room and pick up one balloon at random, look at the name, and return it to its owner. Within minutes, everyone had been reunited with their original balloon.

The speaker then told the group, **"This is what it's like when people are frantically searching for their own happiness in life.** People push others aside to get the things that they want that they believe will bring them happiness. However, our happiness actually lies in helping other people and working together as a community."

Moral:

You will get your happiness if you help other people find theirs. Helping others makes us happy because it gives us a sense of purpose. Helping others brings us happiness for three reasons:

Diversion: When you worry less about your own needs, in this case, finding your own balloon, the stress of that hunt decreases. Taking your focus away from the fact that you can't find your own balloon lets you divert your attention away from your own problem. The feeling of compassion replaces the feeling of need.

Perspective: Having concern for other people helps us remember that we are all facing similar problems in life—no matter what the individual severity of the issue is. Sometimes, when we are focused on our own issues, they get put into perspective when we encounter the true suffering of others (for example, bereavement or a severe disability). It's easy to then realize the excessive amount of attention we've been giving to our own problems. Having compassion helps us put our problems into perspective.

Connection: Connecting with others by helping them can bring happiness into your life. Humans are social beings who need to have positive connections with other people in order to be happy. Connecting with other people enriches our lives and gives us a sense of fulfillment.

Hebrews 13:16

"And do not forget to do good and to share with others,
for with such sacrifices God is pleased."

PRAYER

Heavenly Father,

Please help me to always remember to do good and share with others. May my actions be pleasing to you and may I be a reflection of your love and kindness. Thank you for the opportunity to serve others and bring joy to their lives. All these things I pray in the precious Holy name of Jesus Christ, AMEN.

"The Boulder and the Gold"
(Roald Dahl)

There once was a king who decided to do a little experiment. He had a giant boulder put right in the middle of the street. He then hid near the boulder to see who, if anyone, would try to move it out of the way.

First, some wealthy merchants walked by. They walked around the boulder, complaining that the king hadn't been maintaining the roads very well.

Next, a peasant walked by, heading home with his arms full of food for his family. When he noticed the boulder, he put his groceries down and attempted to move it out of everyone's way. **It took him a while to move it, but he eventually succeeded.** After the peasant gathered up his groceries to carry on home, he noticed a bag lying in the middle of the road, just where the boulder once was. He opened the bag to find that it was stuffed full of gold coins, along with a letter from the king saying that the bag's gold was a reward for the peasant to keep because he had taken the time and energy to move the boulder out of the road for the convenience of others who would be traveling the road in the future.

Moral:

The peasant in this story was taught by the king that every obstacle you face offers an opportunity to improve. If you're able to push through moments that are challenging, you may end up being much better off than you were before you started trying.

This story also offers a lesson in personal responsibility. If you see a job ahead of you, don't leave it for the next person to do. Rather, step up and get the job done to help the people who come after you.

James 1:2-3

"Consider it pure joy, my brothers and sisters,
whenever you face trials of many kinds, because you know that the testing
of your faith produces perseverance."

PRAYER

Dear Heavenly Father,

I desire to grow in grace and become more like Jesus. I am beginning to understand that in this life, I will have tests and trials. I pray that You will keep me steady in the trials of life. I pray that the testing of my faith will develop perseverance in me. I pray that You will refine me in the process. In Jesus' name I pray, AMEN.

"The Chef's Daughter"
(Author Unknown)

Once there was a girl who was complaining to her dad that her life was so hard and that she didn't know how she would get through all of her struggles. She was tired, and she felt like as soon as one problem was solved, another would arise.

Being a chef, the girl's father took her into his kitchen. He boiled three pots of water that were equal in size. He placed potatoes in one pot, eggs in another, and ground coffee beans in the final pot.

He let the pots sit and boil for a while, not saying anything to his daughter.

He turned the burners off after twenty minutes and removed the potatoes from the pot and put them in a bowl. He did the same with the boiled eggs. He then used a ladle to scoop out the boiled coffee and poured it into a mug. He asked his daughter, "What do you see?"

She responded, "Potatoes, eggs, and coffee."

Her father told her to take a closer look and touch the potatoes. After doing so, she noticed they were soft. Her father then told her to break open an egg. She acknowledged the hard-boiled egg. Finally, he told her to take a sip of the coffee. It was rich and delicious.

After asking her father what all of this meant, he explained that each of the three food items had just undergone the exact same hardship–twenty minutes inside of boiling water.

However, each item had a different reaction.

The potato went into the water as a strong, hard item, but after being boiled, it turned soft and weak.

The egg was fragile when it entered the water, with a thin outer shell protecting a liquid interior. However, after it was left to boil, the inside of the egg became firm and strong.

Finally, the ground coffee beans were different. Upon being exposed to boiling water, they changed the water to create something new altogether.

He then asked his daughter, "Which are you? When you face adversity, do you respond by becoming soft and weak? Do you build strength? Or do you change the situation?"

Moral:

Life is full of ups and downs, wins and losses, and big shifts in momentum, and adversity is a big part of this experience. And while many of us would rather not face adversity, it doesn't have to always be a negative thing. In fact, handling adversity can be a positive experience that can lead to personal development.

You choose how you respond to adversity, whether you let it break you down or you stand up in the face of it and learn from it. In many instances, facing adversity gives you a chance to learn important lessons that can help you grow as a person.

When facing adversity, it's important to recognize your freedom to choose how you respond. You can respond in a way that ultimately limits you, or you can choose to have a more productive response that could potentially open windows of opportunity that we didn't know existed. This encourages a positive mindset in the face of hardship, viewing trials as an opportunity for growth and character development through perseverance.

James 1:2-4

"Consider it pure joy, my brothers and sisters, whenever you face trials of many kinds, because you know that the testing of your faith produces perseverance"

PRAYER

Heavenly Father,

Thank you that even in the midst of trials and difficulties, I can find joy, knowing that the testing of my faith produces perseverance within me. Help me embrace these challenges as opportunities to grow in maturity and completeness, trusting that you are working to refine me and make me lack nothing through these experiences. Grant me the strength to endure with patience and faith, knowing that you are with me through every storm. In Jesus' precious name I pray, AMEN.

"The Elephant Rope"
(A.M. Marcus, Shagor Ahamed, and Parshant Thakur)

When walking through an elephant camp, a man noticed that the elephants were only secured with a small rope that was tied around one ankle. He wondered why the elephants didn't break free from the rope, as the elephants were certainly strong enough to do so. He asked a trainer why the elephants didn't try to break free, and the trainer responded by saying that they use the same size rope for baby elephants all the way up to adulthood. Because they're too small when they're babies to break free from the rope, **they grow up being conditioned that the rope is stronger than they are.** As adults, they think the rope can still hold them, so they don't try to fight it.

Moral:

The elephants in this case are experiencing learned helplessness. This phenomenon occurs when someone has been conditioned to anticipate discomfort in some way without having a way to avoid it or make it stop. After enough conditioning, the person will stop any attempts to avoid the pain, even if they see an opportunity to escape.

If you go through life thinking that you can't do something just because you have failed at doing it in the past, you're living with a fixed mindset. You have to let go of your limiting beliefs in order to make the breakthroughs that are required for your ultimate success. Don't let other people tell you that you can't do something, and don't hold onto an assumption that you can't grow and learn from past failures.

Revelation 3:1-2

"These are the words of him who holds the seven spirits of God and the seven stars. I know your deeds; you have a reputation of being alive, but you are dead. Wake up! Strengthen what remains and is about to die, for I have found your deeds unfinished in the sight of my God."

PRAYER

Heavenly Father,

I confess that I may have a reputation for being alive in my faith, but in reality, there are areas where I am spiritually dead. I ask you to wake me up, to strengthen what little remains of my faith, and to renew my commitment to follow You fully. Search my heart and expose any areas where I have become complacent or lukewarm. Help me to return to my first love I had for You and to live my life truly reflecting Your presence in my life. All these things I pray in the precious Holy name of Jesus Christ, AMEN.

"The Little Hero"
(Author Unknown)

There was once a boy who was growing up in a very wealthy family. One day, his father decided to take him on a trip to show him how others, who were less fortunate, lived. His father's goal was to help his son appreciate everything that he had been given in life. The boy and his father pulled up to a farm where a very poor family lived. They spent several days on the farm, helping the family work for their food and take care of their land.

When they left the farm, his dad asked his son if he enjoyed their trip and if he had learned anything during the time they spent with this other family.

The boy quickly replied, **"It was fantastic, that family is so lucky!"**

Confused, his father asked what he meant by that.

The boy said, "Well, we only have one dog, but that family has four, and they have chickens! We have four people in our home, but they have twelve! They have so many people to play with! We have a pool in our yard, but they have a river running through their property. We have lanterns outside so we can see at night, but they have the wide open sky and the beautiful stars to light up their sky. We have a patio, but they have the entire horizon to enjoy; they have endless fields to run around in and play. We have to go to the grocery store, but they are able to grow their own food. Our high fence protects our property and our family, but they don't need such a limiting structure, because their friends protect them."

The father was speechless.

Finally, the boy added, "Thank you for showing me how rich people live, they're so lucky."

Moral:

True wealth and happiness aren't measured by material belongings. Being around the people you love, enjoying the beautiful natural environment God created, and having freedom are much more valuable. A rich life can mean different things to different people. What are your values and priorities? If you have whatever is of the utmost importance to you, you can consider yourself to be wealthy.

Galatians 2:20

"The Spirit is the indwelling wellspring of joy in God that we experience as we live by faith in the Son of God."

PRAYER

Heavenly Father,

I pray that you help me live by faith today. I think about those who are walking through challenges and hurt and suffering right now. God, I pray that You'd help them live by faith in Jesus who loves them and who gave Himself for them. All these things I pray in the precious name of Jesus Christ, AMEN.

"The Professor and the Glass of Water"
(Author Unknown)

A professor raised his glass of water in front of the students. **"How heavy is this glass of water?"** he asked with a smile. The students' answers ranged from 10 to 20 ounces. "Okay. Now, could one of you come here and help me hold the glass?" A girl walked to her table and held the glass. After a few minutes, the girl said, "Sir, I am tired. Is it okay to leave the glass on the table now?" The professor smiled, nodded yes, and said to the students, "Imagine if you have to hold this glass for an hour or even a day! Would you now think that a 10 or 20 ounce weight is too little? "No," all the students answered. "Exactly! Hold it too long and you will only hurt yourself. Always remember to put the glass down several times a day," said the teacher. "The weight of a glass filled with water does not change, but the longer you hold it, the heavier it becomes.

Moral:

Our worries and stresses are like this glass of water. Think about them for a moment, and nothing happens. Think about them longer, and they begin to hurt. Think about them all day long, and you will only feel panic, making you unable to do anything else. Do not carry your burdens all day long, from morning to night. Remember to put your burdens down as often as you can. Remember to put the glass down regularly and take a break during the day.

Matthew 11:28-29

"Come to me, all who are weary and burdened, and I will give you rest. Take my yoke upon you and learn from me, for I am gentle and humble in heart, and you will find rest for your souls."

PRAYER

Heavenly Father,

I come to you today, weary and burdened by the weight of life. Just as You say in Matthew 11:28-29, I "come to You, all you who are weary and burdened, and You will give me rest." I surrender my cares and anxieties to You, asking that You take my yoke upon me and teach me Your ways, for you are gentle and humble in heart. May I find true rest in Your presence, knowing that Your burden is light and Your yoke is easy. In Jesus' precious name, AMEN.

"The Ultimate Gift"
(Author Unknown)

There was once a little girl who desperately needed an emergency blood transfusion to save her life. Her only chance of surviving would be to get a transfusion from her younger brother, who had miraculously overcome the same disease she had, and therefore had antibodies in his blood that were needed to fight the illness.

The doctor explained to the little boy that it would save his sister's life if he were to give her his blood. The boy hesitated for a moment before agreeing to give his blood if it would help his sister. At the age of five, this was a little bit scary, but he would do anything to save his big sister's life.

As the blood transfusion was happening, he lay next to his sister in the hospital and was overcome with happiness as he saw the color coming back to her cheeks. Then he looked up at the doctor and quietly asked, "When will I start to die?"

The boy had assumed that he was giving his life in order to save hers. The little boy's parents were astonished over the misunderstanding that led the boy to think they were choosing his sister over him, and even more astonished that he had agreed to do so. The doctor replied, explaining that he was not going to die; he was just going to allow his sister to live a long, healthy life alongside him.

Moral:

This is an example of extreme courage and self-sacrificing love from a young boy that we can all learn from. The love and care that he showed for his sister relay an inspiring message about selflessness. While we may not be faced with such a life-or-death decision, being selfless in general can help us connect with others, which is rewarding and fulfilling. Selflessness encourages you to act from your heart instead of your ego, and can help fill your life with joy, peace, love, and hope.

*"For when we were still without strength, in due time
Christ died for the ungodly. For scarcely for a righteous man will one die;
yet perhaps for a good man someone would even dare to die. But God
demonstrates His own love toward us, in that while we were still sinners,
Christ died for us."*

PRAYER

Heavenly Father,

I come before You today in awe of Your incredible love, a love so
profound that You sent Your Son, Jesus Christ, to die for me while I was
still a sinner. Thank you that even when I was powerless and considered
Your enemy, Christ died for me, demonstrating the depth of Your grace
and mercy. I praise You for the reconciliation I have through His
sacrifice, and I rejoice in the knowledge that I am now saved by His life,
not just from my sins, but also to live a life fully devoted to You. Help
me to always remember this great gift and to live in the light of Your
love, sharing it with others as I walk in the freedom and hope that comes
from being united with Christ. In Jesus' name, AMEN.

"Three Feet from Gold"
(Napoleon Hill)

During the gold rush, a man who had been mining in Colorado for
several months quit his job, as he hadn't struck gold yet, and the work
was becoming tiresome. He sold his equipment to another man who

resumed mining where it had been left off. The new miner was advised by his engineer that there was gold only three feet away from where the first miner stopped digging. The engineer was right, which means **the first miner was a mere three feet away from striking gold before he quit.**

Moral:

When things start to get hard, try to persevere through the adversity. Many people give up on following their dreams because the work becomes too difficult, tedious, or tiresome, but often, you're closer to the finish line than you may think. If you push just a little harder, you will succeed! Never quit! We are always three feet from Gold. To worry is to pray for what you do NOT want! Before great success comes, you will surely meet with temporary defeat. When people are overtaken by these feelings, the easiest and perhaps most logical thing to do is to quit.

James 1:12

*"Blessed is the one who perseveres under trial because,
having stood the test, that person will receive the crown of life that the
Lord has promised to those who love him."*

PRAYER

Heavenly Father,

In the midst of trials and challenges, I thank you for the promise that 'blessed is the one who perseveres under trial, for when they have stood the test, they will receive the crown of life, which you have promised to those who love you' (James 1:12). Grant me the strength to endure these difficulties with steadfast faith, knowing that my faithfulness will be rewarded with your eternal glory. Guide me through these times, and help me to see beyond the present struggles, focusing on the hope of the crown of life that awaits me. In Jesus' precious and Holy name I pray, AMEN.

"Wait...What?"
(Author Unknown)

A carpenter who was nearing retirement told his boss that he was ready to end his career and spend his time with his wife and family. He would miss his work, but he felt it was time to spend his time with the people who were important to him.

His boss was saddened by this news, as this carpenter had been a good, reliable employee for many years. He asked the carpenter if he could do him a favor and build just one more house.

The carpenter reluctantly conceded, even though his passion for building had faded.

While he was building this last house, his normal work ethic faded, and his efforts were mediocre, at best. He used inexpensive and inferior materials and cut corners wherever he could. It was a poor way to finish such a dedicated thirty-year career he had built.

When the carpenter was finished, his boss came to look at the house. He gave the key to the carpenter and said, "This house is my gift to you for all of the hard work you have done for me over the years." The carpenter was astonished.

What a generous gift this was to receive from his boss, but **if he had known he was building a house for himself, he would have made his usual efforts to create a high-quality home.**

Moral:

The same idea applies to how you build your life. Every day that you wake up offers an opportunity for you to put your best foot forward, yet we often do mediocre work, saving the more important things for "another" day. Then one day, we find ourselves shocked that our lives aren't what we had hoped they would be. The "structure" we built to live in has a lot of flaws due to a lack of effort and an extreme sense of apathy.

Matthew 7:24-27

"Therefore everyone who hears these words of mine and puts them into practice is like a wise man who built his house on the rock. The rain came down, the streams rose, and the winds blew and beat against that house; yet it did not fall, because it had its foundation on the rock. But everyone who hears these words of mine and does not put them into practice is like a foolish man who built his house on sand. The rain came down, the streams rose, and the winds blew and beat against that house, and it fell with a great crash."

PRAYER
Heavenly Father,

Thank You for Your wisdom and guidance. Just as the wise man built his house on a rock, I pray that You would establish my life on a firm foundation of Your word. Help me to not just hear Your teachings but to actively live them out, so that when storms of life come, my faith will not crumble. Strengthen me to resist temptation and choose Your path, always remembering that true security comes from building my life on the solid rock of Your love. In Jesus' name I pray, AMEN.

"Walking on Water"
(Author Unknown)

Once there was a boy who lived with his family on a farm. They had a beautiful dog who would go down to the pond for hours every day in the spring and summer with the boy to practice retrieving various items. The boy wanted to prepare his dog for any scenario that may come up during duck season because he wanted his dog to be the best hunting dog in the whole county.

The boy and his dog had vigorous training sessions every day until the dog was so obedient, he wouldn't do anything unless he was told to do so by the boy.

As duck season rolled in with the fall and winter months, the boy and his dog were eager to be at their regular spot down at the pond near their house. Only a few minutes passed before the two heard the first group of ducks flying overhead. The boy slowly raised his gun and shot three times before killing a duck, which landed in the center of the pond.

When the boy signaled his dog to retrieve the duck, the dog charged through the duck blind and bushes toward the pond. However, instead of swimming in the water like he had practiced so many times, the dog walked on the water's surface, retrieved the duck, and returned it to the boy.

The boy was astonished. His dog had an amazing ability to walk on water—it was like magic. The boy knew no one would ever believe this amazing thing that he had just witnessed. He had to get someone else down there to see this incredible phenomenon.

The boy went to a nearby farmer's house and asked if he would hunt with him the next morning. The neighbor agreed and met up with the boy the following morning at his regular spot by the pond.

The pair patiently waited for a group of ducks to fly overhead, and soon enough, they heard them coming. The boy told the neighbor to go ahead and take a shot, which the neighbor did, killing one duck. Just as the day before, the boy signaled to his dog to fetch the duck. Miraculously, the dog walked on the water again to retrieve the duck.

The boy was bursting with pride and could hardly contain himself when he asked his neighbor, "Did you see that? What do you think?!"

The neighbor responded, "I wasn't going to say anything, but your dog doesn't even know how to swim."

The boy sat in disbelief as his neighbor **pointed out a potential flaw in the dog rather than recognizing the fact that what he had just done was a miracle.**

Moral:

People will often downplay others' abilities or achievements because they're unable to accomplish the same thing. Don't let this bring you down. Just move on and keep working on improving yourself.

Maintaining a positive mindset is a key part of being successful. Furthermore, be conscious of instances in which you may be tempted to not give credit where it is deserved. Rejoice in other people's accomplishments and lift them up with praise. Pointing out other people's shortcomings does not make you a better person. Believe in yourself and believe in others. Be an encouragement to all.

Hebrews 3:13

"But encourage one another daily, as long as it is called 'Today,' so that none of you may be hardened by sin's deceitfulness."

PRAYER

Heavenly Father,

When I am uncertain about what I should do, show me Your ways. When I don't know which way to turn, teach me and show me. In everything I do, I ask You to guide me. I want to trust You, and I ask that You would protect me. Lord, help me surround myself with positive believers, emphasizing the need for mutual encouragement and accountability amongst us. In Jesus' name I pray, AMEN.

"What a Waste"
(Author Unknown)

A mother camel and her baby were lying down, soaking up the sun. The baby camel asked his mom, "Why do we have these big bumps on our backs?"

The mom stopped to think and then said, "We live in the desert where there is not much water available. Our humps store water to help us survive on long journeys."

The baby camel then stopped to think and said, "Well, why do we have long legs with rounded feet?"

His mother replied, "They are meant to help us walk through sand."

The baby asked a third question, "Why are my eyelashes so long?"

The mother replied, "Your long eyelashes offer you protection from sand when it blows in the wind."

Finally, the baby said, **"If we have all of these natural abilities given to us to walk through the desert, what's the use for camels in the zoo?"**

Moral:

The skills and abilities that you possess won't be useful if you're not in the right environment. You've probably heard of a professional who left his or her career to follow their dreams, or the person who remains unfulfilled in their job, but doesn't try to make a change. If you're stuck in a career that isn't the right fit, you have to do some self-reflection to realize where your strengths lie that are going to waste. Turn to people that you know the best, as well as professionals in any given area, so you can start thinking about what you may be most passionate about and naturally good at.

Romans 12:6-8

"We have different gifts, according to the grace given to each of us. If your gift is prophesying, then prophesy in accordance with your faith; if it is serving, then serve; if it is teaching, then teach;

if it is to encourage, then give encouragement; if it is giving, then give generously; if it is to lead, do it diligently; if it is to show mercy, do it cheerfully."

PRAYER

Heavenly Father,

Thank you for the diverse gifts You have bestowed upon me, according to your grace. Guide me to discover and embrace my unique abilities, whether it be to prophesy with boldness, serve with humility, teach with clarity, encourage with compassion, give generously, lead with wisdom, or show mercy with cheerfulness. Help me to use these gifts not for personal gain, but to build up Your Church and reflect Your love to the world. May I always use my talents to uplift others and bring glory to Your name. In Jesus' precious Holy name I pray, AMEN.

"Will You Marry Me?"
(Author Unknown)

Centuries ago, in a small Italian town, there was a business owner who was in a great amount of debt. His banker, who was an old, unattractive man, strongly desired the business owner's younger, beautiful daughter. The banker decided to offer the businessman a deal to forgive the debt that he owed the bank completely. However, there was a bit of a catch.

In order for the businessman to become debt-free, he was to have his daughter marry the banker. The businessman didn't want to concede to this agreement, but he had no other choice, as his debt was so extreme.

The banker said he would put two small stones into a bag—one of which was white, and the other black. The daughter would then need to reach into the bag and blindly choose a stone. If she chose the black stone, the businessman's debt would be cleared, and the daughter would have to marry the banker. However, if she chose the white stone, the debt would be cleared, and the daughter would not have to marry him.

While standing in the stone-filled path in the businessman's yard, the banker reached down and chose two small stones, not realizing that the businessman's daughter was watching him. **She noticed that he picked up two black stones and put them in the bag.**

When it came time for the daughter to pick a stone out of the bag, she felt she had two choices: Refuse to do it. Take out both stones and expose the banker's cheating.

Pick a stone, knowing it would be black, and sacrifice herself to get her father out of debt.

She picked a stone from the bag, and immediately 'accidentally' dropped it into the abundance of stones where they were all standing. She said to the banker, "I'm sorry, I'm so clumsy! Oh well. Just look in the bag to see what color stone is already in there, so you will know what color stone I picked."

Of course, the remaining stone was black. Because the banker didn't want his deceit to be exposed, he played along, acting as if the stone that the businessman's daughter dropped had to have been white. He cleared the businessman's debt, and the daughter remained free from having to spend the rest of her life with the banker.

Moral:

While you may have to think outside of the box sometimes, it's always possible to conquer a difficult situation. You don't have to always give in to the options you're presented with. Challenge the status quo. Think creatively. Engage in productive nonconformity when possible. Don't be afraid to question the things that are expected to be true. In order to overcome challenges, you have to think in ways that you've never thought before. Get out of your comfort zone and discover a newfound freedom that you have never experienced before.

Joshua 1:9

"Have I not commanded you? Be strong and courageous. Do not be afraid; do not be discouraged, for the Lord your God will be with you wherever you go."

PRAYER

Heavenly Father,

Please give me strength, courage, and guidance in the face of fear, adversity, and uncertainty. Help me rely on You and find my hope in Your promises. Help me be strong and courageous and not afraid or discouraged. I trust that You will be with me wherever I go. All these things I pray in the precious Holy name of Jesus Christ, AMEN.

Final Story of God's Providence:
Faith & Pain & Humility

Carmen K. Maendel

Cancer Diagnosis: Basal-Cell Skin Cancer

I had a recent scare with a diagnosis of basal-cell skin cancer in multiple areas on my body. On the evening of November 5th, I asked Nate about a small pink fleshy mound that seemed to be growing on my leg. He was previously an LPN nurse and told me to get in to see our doctor immediately. I was able to be seen the very next day, and our family doctor took one look at my leg and the two spots on my back and recommended that I see our dermatologist immediately. This is how God works. Usually, it is impossible to see our family doctor for months as he is booked out over time with many patients. He saw me, and then I was also able to sneak in to see the dermatologist the very next day due to a cancellation. I went to the dermatologist thinking that they were just going to do a full body skin check and be done. I have always watched for dark spots or moles that change color or shape; however, I was not ready for what the dermatologist said next: "We need to do biopsies immediately on all three spots, and we will let you know if they are benign or cancerous in the next few days." I had the biopsies done, and those next three days were excruciatingly long waiting for what was next. I got the call, and my heart sank as they told me that all three spots were basal-cell skin cancer. I have lost many relatives on my dad's side, including my father to cancer, and I literally freaked out. I now had to wait until December 9th and 30th for both of my surgeries to remove the cancer from my body. This whole past month of November, I felt numb, distracted, and just downright defeated. You see, because of my family genes with cancer on my dad's side and strokes and diabetes on my mom's side, I have gone to great lengths to protect my health with healthy nutrition and regular exercise over the years. All I could do was wait, be still, and worry about how much cancer could be in my body already. I was awaiting the results of a Cologuard test and mammogram as well. I had allowed fear to replace my faith in God, and that alone placed me in a paralyzed state.

Finally, I received word on both the Cologuard and mammogram that they were negative, and this nightmare I was envisioning of cancer attacking my entire body could be laid to rest. I certainly was not out of the woods yet, though. One set of tests done, and I still had to go into surgery on December 9th to have the cancer removed from my leg. My doctor went deep and covered a larger area to make sure that she got all of it the first time. I remember going into the office that day. I had worn a velour tracksuit that the leg could be pushed up to avoid having to wear one of those ridiculous hospital gowns. I was so thankful that my husband took off work for our company and went with me that day. Just having him there made everything easier for me to handle the entire surgery that day. I remember they had me lie down and prick me with needles for the lidocaine to numb the area they were going to do surgery on. I really wish they had knocked me out completely. Something about being aware that they are removing skin tissue on my leg and leaving a hole there did not sit well with me. I tried to be a good sport, and I was super blessed with both my nurse and doctor that day. I had explained to them both that I had an extreme amount of anxiety about this whole process. I explained that cancer had run on my dad's side, and strokes and diabetes on my mom's, so I did not exactly win the genetic lottery in that respect. That is one of the largest reasons that I became a Certified Fitness Trainer and got my Master's in Nutrition and DNA Testing and Analysis. I wanted to be in the best shape of my life in case something ever happened to me with my health. I was faced with COVID-19 pneumonia in 2021 and now cancer in 2024. Weeks prior, I remember sharing this news with my church women's Bible study and breaking down in tears. So many unknowns, and the word itself, CANCER, has always scared me! All my closest friends were very supportive during this time. I had a number of them who checked in with me daily and sent encouraging Scripture to my phone. I remember attending Thanksgiving with our family in the cities, and for whatever reason it was, I did not share this with any of them. Perhaps it simply was not the right time or place, or I did not want to ruin the cool vibe by celebrating with our family. I did share with my mother-in-law and one sister-in-law, who I am super close to, and they were extremely supportive during this time.

So here I was, face down and getting pricks in my legs to prep me for the upcoming surgery on my leg. Part of the reason I was freaking out is that I could not recall how long I had seen this pink fleshy thing that I thought was simply a small injury that had not healed properly. My doctor had informed me that basal-cell skin cancer is the least aggressive form of skin cancer; however, if left untreated, it can metastasize to the bone and cause death. Tears started streaming down my face, and I was not sure if they were from the pain of the pricks or the fear of the unknown. My doctor and nurse were extremely patient and supportive of me and explained the entire procedure to me. Eventually, my leg got numb, and I was oblivious to the rest of the procedure. It was not until the lidocaine wore off that I realized how painful my leg felt. One caveat I forgot to mention is that one week prior to my going into surgery, I slipped and caught myself (without actually falling) on our bathroom floor and tweaked my back. Like I said before, I was in a pretty dark place and feeling somewhat defeated when it came to my health. I have always been a healthy individual, and this was definitely a humbling experience that God was walking me through at this time. I remember I had alternated icing my back and heating it for twenty minutes while lying on our massage pad. After a full day of about twelve cycles of each, I had not gotten better. I really tweaked my back badly this time, and it was just going to take some time to heal. There was one trip to the E.R. One evening, my entire body started shaking, and both Nate and I were not sure if it was a sign of shock. They checked me out and sent me home with a muscle relaxer that helped heal my back and the uncontrollable spasms I was having at that time.

It took about a week for my back to heal, and I was able to make it to my leg surgery. The surgery was successful, and I am blessed to have my husband, who has previous medical knowledge, dress my leg wound daily for me. I tried not to complain even when it hurt as he cleaned it with hydrogen peroxide, placed Vaseline on the wound, and bandaged it up again each day. I feel blessed that God has given me this experience, even if it was not all positive. I still have surgery for the two spots on my back scheduled for the 30th of December 2024. My doctor reassured me that these spots are a level zero basal-cell skin cancer and will be nowhere near as invasive to remove as my leg surgery was. I received a call on December 9th that made my day. The dermatology clinic called and let me know over the phone that I did not have to come in again for my leg, and the pathologist stated that we got all the cancer in one hit! I needed a win at this time. Also, the following day, I received my solo book offer through She Rises Studios and Fenix TV, and I officially signed that day to write this book. God works in mysterious ways. One day, I am having cancer dug out of my leg, and the next, I am offered a solo book deal. This is yet another example of how God takes something negative and turns it around for good. God is faithful in all His promises, and He never changes yesterday, today, or in the future.

The remainder of the basal-cell skin cancer surgery, removing two spots on my back, was very minor compared to my leg; however, there was a healing period for those wounds on my back as well. My back surgery was superficial, with my doctor cauterizing the areas and then simply scraping them off. My doctor also checked on the progress of my leg healing up at this time. Everything seemed to be healing up properly at this visit. My doctor applied a medication, twice now, on my wound to kill the extra tissue and blood cells as the wound heals from the bottom up. The wound is much less deep and appears to be starting to close up nicely. My last follow-up appointment on my leg is three weeks from today. I have been incredibly blessed to have my husband clean and dress my wound daily through this entire process. His former LPN certification and experience working in a hospital have surely been a blessing to me, and my doctor commented on how clean and professional he has been keeping my wounds since the day of my surgery. One more example of the way God has worked in my life through transforming something bad to good, and placing those around me that I need the most to be able to recover from all this. I had amazing doctors and nurses, and my husband took care of me at home. Even with the pain and discomfort of the cleaning and bandaging of three wounds daily, I look at this experience now as a true blessing. I will be changing my lifestyle in the following ways: 1) boating only with a canopy to shield me from the sun, 2) outdoor sports with a spray sunscreen on at all times, and 3) no more lying out in the sun at the beach during summer for me (beach trips under a tree or an umbrella only from this day forward). I am also required, by my doctor, to come in every six months for the rest of my life for full-body skin checks just to stay on top of things. I am truly thankful this was not worse than it was, and that they removed 100% of the cancer from my body. God healed me. I remember, in retrospect, thinking and feeling that something just did not feel right with my body, and I was unable to put my finger on what was wrong at that time. I truly believe that was God nudging me in the direction to go have things checked out medically, and I am so glad that I did. I usually am very in tune with my body, and I knew something was not quite right. God opened the doors for all the dermatology appointments, dates for my surgeries, incredible doctor and nurse staff, and for my husband to take care of me as I healed over a period of time at home.

The small amount of discomfort I felt going through this entire experience is nowhere near the pain and anguish that Jesus experienced dying on the cross for all of our sins. I have learned to thank Jesus for the valleys and the mountain tops in life, and realize I can not truly appreciate one without the other. I learned not to waste the experiences that God gives me in life for a reason. There is a reason that I went through this painful experience, and I may not understand all the specifics "why" on this side of heaven. I have learned to trust God with 100% of my life and the experiences I have on this earth. I believe this experience was given to me in order to help me rely 100% on Him and not on the things of this world. I also realize that I have no control over these things that occur in my life, and that is okay. The overwhelming "peace" that comes when you fully submit to God's will and plan for your life is absolutely priceless!

Philippians 4:7

"And the peace of God, which passeth all understanding,
shall guard your hearts and your thoughts in Christ Jesus."

Romans 8:16-17

"The Spirit Himself bears witness with our spirit that we are
children of God, and if children, then heirs—heirs of God and joint heirs
with Christ, if indeed we suffer with Him,
that we may also be glorified together."

Carmen Maendel

COURAGEOUS WOMAN CASTING
CARES UPON JESUS

Powered by ◀▶ MySignature.io

MEET THE AUTHOR
WHO IS CARMEN MAENDEL?

I am a child of God. I am created in His image, and apart from Him, I am nothing! My identity lies in Christ alone, and I really feel like God has led me to help women. **I am also a wife.** I met my husband in Colorado Springs back in 2005 at the singles group, Mosaic, that we both attended. Nate and I are going on eighteen years of marriage this coming July. **I am a mother.** We were blessed with our son, Joshua, in January 2009. He is a wonderful, loving, very precocious sixteen-year-old today who loves his newfound freedom in driving his own truck now. **I am a friend.** I take my friendships very seriously, and I do not have many close friends. However, I have deep relationships with the ones I do have. **I was a coach.** I coached over fifty women for eight years in our gym, Maendel Fitness. It was such an honor to come alongside these women and help them lose weight, build muscle, gain core strength, and learn how to do HIIT Cardio and Strength Training exercises. **I love to connect business professionals to each other.** I love being able to help business professionals connect with and form collaborations with other business professionals, especially in the area of women. **I love to lift up women.** I love connecting women to other women in a business and personal setting. I created and hosted BNO (Beauties Night Out) for six years, and I started LNO (Ladies Night Out) in our church around three years ago. We get together with 7th graders and up to pray and encourage each other in various activities for ladies fellowship, the last Friday of the month from 6 to 9 p.m. **I am a student for life**; I never quit learning! I love to learn about a variety of different topics every opportunity that I get in life. **I am passionate about health and fitness** and constantly looking up new information in this field, even if I am not coaching women professionally anymore. **I am an entrepreneur.** I founded Maendel Fitness in 2016 and owned/co-owned several companies prior to that as well. Maendel Fitness and online program Rock Hard Body (Power, Strength & Fitness) were successful from 2016 to 2023 until I was forced to close both due to an "almost" move our family made outside of this area. **I am a cook.** I love to cook with my son and husband, and my hubby, Nate, is way better at the grill than I am. Our son is a very good cook as well, and we enjoy experimenting with new ethnic foods and variations of dishes together. **I am a photographer.** I actually owned a photography business prior to Maendel Fitness (Carmen Maendel Photography); however, it's more of a hobby for me now. I certainly enjoy picking up my camera and being able to capture those amazing moments in life. **I am a boater.** Our family loves to go out on the lake, especially when it is super hot. We love to zoom around the lake for a little while, and then stop in the center to dive right in to cool off. **I am an adventure seeker.** I love to go on adventures with those I am close to. I am always open to learning new things and experiencing new opportunities in life. **I am a world traveler.** My husband and I have traveled to Mexico four times, to Cancun twice, Playa del Carmen and the Riviera Maya area with our son once. Nate and I also spent our tenth wedding anniversary in five different regions of Italy (the Island of Murano, Venice, Florence, Tuscany, and Rome). I also did some traveling in Europe (England, France, and Spain) myself before I even met my husband; I studied in Valladolid, Spain, for a summer as well. **I am a horse lover.** I grew up in the country with horses, and absolutely love everything about horses and the country lifestyle. I showed my Tennessee Walker, Ed, in 4H as a kid, and my husband and I share the dream of owning our own horse ranch someday in the future. **I was a sports and fitness model.** I have had the opportunity to do some sports and fitness modeling in this industry since I opened Maendel Fitness in 2016. **I am a motivator.** I love to motivate and encourage others. I encouraged my clients when I was training them, and I still to this day love to encourage everyone I meet. **I love the outdoors.** Hiking, biking, swimming, volleyball, jogging, broomball, riding horses, and basically any outdoor activity I am game for. I love to play sports outside with friends with a competitive, friendly approach. **I am an author.** I have recently written in ten anthologies with other amazing women around the world, and this book is my first solo book with She Rises Studios and Fenix TV. This is me in a nutshell!

Carmen Maendel is a talented, courageous woman of God expressing herself as a poet through her publication of "Enigma," copyrighted 2006, and author of an online fitness program: Rock Hard Body in 2022. She has owned/co-owned and operated four businesses in the past twelve years (Genoa Denim and Leather Apparel, Carmen Maendel Photography, and Maendel Fitness Gym & Spa) and currently co-owns and operates Nate's Property Maintenance LLC with her husband, Nate Maendel. Prior to this, she taught English and Math in Special Education for five years and had a successful eight-year career as a Stockbroker and Financial Advisor with Edward D. Jones and JP Morgan Chase.

Carmen, in conjunction with a close friend, Traci Galles, launched and operated Genoa Denim & Leather Apparel in 2012. These ladies were published in the Brainerd Dispatch Paper by Renee Richardson on August 17, 2012, for their creative and innovative company. Despite the failure of the transfer of this company to the online space, they were able to sell it to Underground Apparel that same year for a profit.

Carmen's creative edge blossoms in her poem "Enigma" and her showcase piece, "A Little Loony" for Carmen Maendel Photography. "Enigma" was published in Timeless Voices, The International Library of Poetry Editor's Choice Series, copyrighted in 2006, and it depicts the deep mysteries and anticipations about the innocence of growing up. "A Little Loony" has been recognized in worldwide photography contests from 2013 to the present, and continues to stand out as her masterpiece photograph of all time.

Carmen created and launched an online program, Rock Hard Body, in 2022, in which she encapsulated all the training and coaching she had done at the Maendel Fitness Gym for the last eight years with over fifty women. She overcame her own fears and broke through barriers, producing this program with the guidance and coaching of James Allen and Mercile Martinsen. She has inspired women all over the world to discover their spiritual sides and crush obstacles blocking their path to their freedom and goals.

Today, Carmen enjoys using the talents and gifting God has given her to complement her husband's talents and gifting in owning and operating Nate's Property Maintenance LLC. They are a husband and wife team, and run a professional and efficient business together with their team of workers. Carmen handles all business on the home front, and Nate coordinates all the intricacies of their tree projects with their clients and crew on the job sites. Nate and Carmen enjoy family time boating, hiking, vacationing overseas, and doing various outdoor activities during their downtime. They continue to view their business as a service and value the depth of the relationships they form with their clientele. Carmen has recently contributed her authorship with She Rises Studios and Fenix TV, writing chapters for ten different books, and is a debut author with her solo book, Courageous Woman: Casting Cares Upon Jesus.

LinkedIn: https://www.linkedin.com/in/carmen-maendel-17510944/
Facebook: https://www.facebook.com/ncmaendel
Instagram: https://www.instagram.com/maendelcarmen/
Websites:
natespropertymaintenance.com
courageouswoman.net

JOIN THE MOVEMENT

#Courageouswoman.net

Pay It Forward & Spread the Word!!!

With Carmen K. Maendel

Courageous Woman Casting Cares Upon Jesus was written after Carmen K. Maendel was obedient to God's calling for her to write this book. She is praying and waiting to see what God has for her next.

courageouswoman.net was created as a safe place for people to learn about Carmen's Faith Journey and ask for prayer, order books that encourage them in their own faith journeys, and inquire about Carmen coming to speak at their particular venue or stage.

To learn more information,
email: info@courageouswoman.net

RESOURCES & INDEX

Carmen Maendel

COURAGEOUS WOMAN CASTING
CARES UPON JESUS

Powered by  MySignature.io